PERGAMON INTERNATIONAL LIBRARY
of Science, Technology, Engineering and Social Studies
*The 1000-volume original paperback library in aid of
education, industrial training and the enjoyment of leisure*
Publisher: Robert Maxwell, M.C.

The Aesthetic Impulse

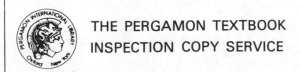

THE PERGAMON TEXTBOOK
INSPECTION COPY SERVICE

An inspection copy of any book published in the Pergamon International Library will
gladly be sent to academic staff without obligation for their consideration for course adoption
or recommendation. Copies may be retained for a period of 60 days from receipt and returned
if not suitable. When a particular title is adopted or recommended for adoption for class use
and the recommendation results in a sale of 12 or more copies, the inspection copy may be
retained with our compliments. The Publishers will be pleased to receive suggestions for
revised editions and new titles to be published in this important International Library.

Other Pergamon titles of interest

Curriculum Issues in Arts Education – *Edited by* Malcolm Ross

Volume 1   The Arts and Personal Growth

Volume 2   The Aesthetic Imperative

Volume 3   The Development of Aesthetic Experience

Volume 4   The Arts: A Way of Knowing

Related Journals

Evaluation in Education

Studies in Educational Evaluation

The
Aesthetic Impulse

by
MALCOLM ROSS
University of Exeter, U.K.

PERGAMON PRESS
OXFORD · NEW YORK · TORONTO · SYDNEY · PARIS · FRANKFURT

U.K.	Pergamon Press Ltd., Headington Hill Hall, Oxford OX3 0BW, England
U.S.A.	Pergamon Press Inc., Maxwell House, Fairview Park, Elmsford, New York 10523, U.S.A.
CANADA	Pergamon Press Canada Ltd., Suite 104, 150 Consumers Rd., Willowdale, Ontario M2J 1P9, Canada
AUSTRALIA	Pergamon Press (Aust.) Pty. Ltd., P.O. Box 544, Potts Point, N.S.W. 2011, Australia
FRANCE	Pergamon Press SARL, 24 rue des Ecoles, 75240 Paris, Cedex 05, France
FEDERAL REPUBLIC OF GERMANY	Pergamon Press GmbH, Hammerweg 6, D–6242 Kronberg-Taunus, Federal Republic of Germany

First edition 1984

Library of Congress Cataloging in Publication Data

Ross, Malcolm, 1932–
The Aesthetic Impulse
(Pergamon international library of science,
technology, engineering, and social studies.
Bibliography: p.148
1. Arts—Study and teaching. I. Title. II. Series
NX294.R67   1984   700' .7 83–17420

British Library Cataloguing in Publication Data

Ross, M.
The Aesthetic Impulse
I. Title
700' 1   BH39

ISBN 0–08–030234–3 (Hardcover)
      0–08–030233–5 (Flexicover)

Printed in Great Britain by A. Wheaton & Co. Ltd., Exeter

TO MY MOTHER

"T'our bodies turn we then, and so
Weak men on love reveal'd may look,
Loves mysteries in souls do grow,
And yet the body is the book."

JOHN DONNE, *The Ecstasy*

Preface

In this essay I want to try to give wider currency to the word "*aesthetic*" as describing a significant area of the school curriculum that would include but not be confined to the creative arts. In doing so I shall propose that the central value of the arts in education is aesthetic – in short that the aim of arts education is the *qualification of sensibility*. That the *arts* are primarily committed to the development of intelligent feeling. Art itself is what philosophers like to call a "contested" concept, and artists seek various, even contradictory goals in their own practice. I believe the central concern of arts education however, obvious though such a statement might seem, has to be with the arts rather than say with the child's social or moral development. The arts are important to a child's education because they are a way of knowing in their own right and offer unique access to certain dimensions of human experience.

I am not being merely pedantic here. I think I can perhaps clarify my position by distinguishing what I have in mind from two currently popular alternative views. Such views emphasize the "academic" and the "instrumental" value of education in or through the arts and are in my terms concerned with outcomes that are strictly extra-aesthetic. Their hope is to make the arts legitimate by aligning them with the so-called "core" curriculum. The stance of the arts educator is critical for it is projected into a particular kind of teaching and, of course, seeks and rewards certain kinds of educational outcomes rather than others. For my own part I shall want to insist that the "poetic" or "cultural" experience of art has to be the basis of any statement about the nature and purpose of a general arts education.

The school curriculum is constituted of three principal fields of learning – or, to put it another way, is directed towards three complementary kinds of outcome: the academic, the practical or instrumental and the cultural. The academic curriculum introduces children to the world of "pure" knowledge and to the rewards of scholarship. The practical curriculum is designed to equip children with the technical skills and know-how that will fit them for employment and for their role in society: its criteria are essentially economic, as are its intended rewards. The cultural curriculum, by no means as readily identifiable in most schools, seeks to help children grow as persons, as individuals within society. Its rewards are intrinsic and immediate rather than, as with the other two areas already alluded to, deferred. The individual child learns about himself or herself, develops what we might call "personal knowledge", acquires a sense of values and the ability to cope with the experience of "being in the world".

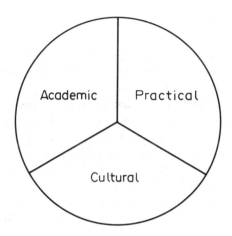

If such an analysis applies to the curriculum as a whole – it can also be applied to any particular subject area within it. For instance it is usual to distinguish between the pure and the applied fields of mathematics and science. I would maintain that the aesthetic area is no exception. My point is that under the present extreme economic circumstances that we are experiencing it is possible to discern noticeable tendencies to pull arts education back from too close an identification with the more nebulous dimension of "culture" and to negotiate a new legitimacy as an aspect either of the academic (pure) or the practical (applied) core.

In a recent article (see Ross, 1982) Gavin Bolton writing about drama in education exemplifies what I call the instrumental approach to arts education. He is, of course, by no means a lone voice. I sense for instance that an instrumental view of arts education informs a good deal in the Gulbenkian Foundation Report "The Arts in Schools". Writing about drama as learning Bolton is not especially concerned that much of what goes on in drama lessons could not be categorised as art. Drama can be a "fine education" nevertheless and he gives two reasons:

> "One is that dramatic method is potentially so educationally rich that experience falling short of art can still be hugely beneficial. And secondly, linked with the first, it is possible that pupils even at secondary level may not acquire the necessary skills to create a group artistic product and yet still have a worthwhile course." (p. 145).

Bolton is not necessarily guilty of substituting non-aesthetic criteria in such an evaluation: he may simply not wish to call what children do "art", or prefer to attach value to art as process rather than product. I confess I'm not too sure. However the notion that drama can be a fine education whilst having nothing to do with art worries me a very great deal and, narrow as I may appear in saying so, it is a view from which I want to be wholly dissociated. For me drama in education is an occasion for aesthetic learning: it is utterly trivialized when defined merely as a pedagogic device (no matter how rich).

The academic case is well illustrated in a recent paper by the art critic Andrew Brighton. Writing in *Aspects*, No. 18, Spring 1982, Brighton attacked secondary art education as sloppy and undisciplined. He complained that unless it were possible completely to re-think what art education should be about at the secondary level then tertiary art education would become primarily "a form of remedial teaching". He lamented the influence of writers such as Herbert Read and Robert Witkin disapproving thoroughly of what he called their misplaced enthusiasm for a "paltry creativity". His own view is that we should

> "...teach and evaluate that which can be taught and evaluated, that is, skills and knowledge."

Brighton argues for what he describes as "a new academicism" in art education. One of the principal problems with his paper that I find is that he seems to confuse general with specialist art education in schools – perhaps a general education in art would be incomprehensible to him anyway. However that may be, he speaks for a growing faction in education in castigating the creative expressionists and so-called mystics. Intending readers of this volume are warned that it is specifically directed against both the new academicism and the new pragmatism in arts education.

I suspect it is over the character of the aesthetic educational encounter itself that Brighton would most strenuously wish to disagree with me. And I hasten to add that plenty of arts teachers will also disagree with me, though perhaps on different grounds. Read and Witkin are both committed to the principle of education as experience, rather than, for instance, as study. To "knowing" rather than to "knowing about". My own views are possibly even more extreme. What intrigues me most about trying to develop the expressive responses of my own students – children and adults – is what David Jones refers to as the *sacred* dimension of the aesthetic. I am not speaking here specifically either of religious or of moral values, though I daresay what I have in mind could be accommodated by the word "spiritual". I am thinking of the power inherent in human perception of finding sensuous objects numinous. Although I readily admit that the practices of both creation and appreciation require conscious as well as unconscious control, knowledge and technical skills as well as expressive impulse, I feel my central task is to try and create what Gaston Bachelard calls the conditions of the daydream, and to help my students establish firm and sensitive ties between their formative feelings and the materials and artifacts which they encounter. It is arguably rather easier to teach the skills and knowledge about "the artifacts of Western and other cultures". Brighton is of course prepared to give his art curriculum a strongly practical emphasis, but – so it seems to me – is determined that it should be product and convention centred. Whereas for me, as for Witkin, the heart of the experience is impulse. Only impulse can give a child's expressive experience particular and personal significance. My own experience is that of all the skills I most need, activating and sustaining children's expressive actions causes me the most headaches and most reveals my limitations as their teacher. I shall not here rehearse either Witkin's reactive/reflexive distinction, or repeat his argument about working within the pupil's expressive act. (Witkin, 1974).

My concern for the spiritual, for the sacredness, the sacramental character of art is admittedly selective and partial. But then I feel entitled to make this kind of choice – provided of course that I'm also prepared to confess to and discuss it. Art in general education has to be selective: time, resources, opportunities are strictly (even damagingly) restricted and it's a question of deciding which kind of a message, above all, one wants to leave impressed upon the students' minds. Of course a more specialized curriculum, designed with vocational ends in view, would be built upon different principles. Selective also of course, as Brighton's own programme cannot avoid being. I am not in much doubt about what I want my students to remember about their sessions with me, especially when I take into account the all-pervading secularity and the sterile academicism of the curriculum (in school, college and university) as a whole. I am persuaded that the function of the arts in general education is to give children – by whatever means and in whatever medium – experiences of the sacred and of the numinous. Not information but experience.

I might have used two other words equally well: *liminality* and *communitas*. Victor W. Turner in his book *The Ritual Process* uses these terms to describe those cultural experiences associated, in so-called primitive societies, with initiation and other transitional rites (rites de passage). Of the condition of liminality he writes:

> "The attributes of liminality or of liminal *personae* (threshold people) are necessarily ambiguous, since this condition and these people elude or slip through the network of classifications that normally locate states and positions in cultural space. Liminal entities are neither here nor there; they are betwixt and between the positions assigned and arranged by law, custom, convention and ceremonial".

I go on in this book to lay considerable emphasis upon the "otherness" of art.

The concept of communitas is perhaps a little more difficult – but in essence it bespeaks a social relationship of equals, united by a deep bond of feeling, as is common among ritual participants, in a de-differentiated sense of wholeness, oneness, continuity. It may best be appreciated if contrasted with the concept to which it is most strictly opposed: the status-bound character of ordinary social structures. Turner goes on to argue that our lives need a balance of structure and impulse, the sacred and the secular. (It occurs to me that one of the reasons the Community Arts idea seems doomed might be the failure to recognize that where the arts are concerned communitas is of more significance than community).

> "Spontaneous communitas has something magical about it. Subjectively there is in it the feeling of endless power. But this power untransformed cannot readily be applied to the organizational details of social existence. It is no substitute for lucid thought and sustained will. On the other hand, structural action swiftly becomes arid and mechanical if those involved in it are not periodically immersed in *the regenerative abyss of communitas*". (my italics)

Art lessons in general education should be principally concerned with this immersion in the "regenerative abyss". I strongly doubt the appeal of such a principle to either Bolton or Brighton.

Turner contrasts liminality with the status system in terms of a series of binary oppositions or discriminations. I won't give his complete list but the following selection will be sufficient to indicate the orientation of my own work in arts education.

> "Transition/state
> Totality/partiality
> Homogeneity/heterogeneity
> Communitas/structure
> Equality/inequality
> Anonymity/systems of nomenclature
> Sacredness/secularity
> Absence of status/status
> Nakedness or uniform clothing/distinctions of clothing
> Silence/speech
> Foolishness/sagacity
> Minimization of sex distinctions/sex discrimination
> Humility/just pride of position
> Disregard for personal appearance/care for personal appearance
> Unselfishness/selfishness
> Simplicity/complexity
> Acceptance of pain and suffering/avoidance of pain and suffering"
> (Full list, *The Ritual Process*, pp. 92, 93)

I hope I may have said enough at least to have given some indication of the kind of encounter I think appropriate to a general arts course. I may seem, already, to have plunged the argument into the hottest of waters. For there will be some arts educators, especially perhaps those of the "instrumentalist" persuasion, who will see in this bias of mine nothing more nor less than the old "art for art's sake" tradition. Will take me as saying that children should learn about art, practise and respond to art, because art is its own reward, its own justification. By implication, and in its extreme form, art as a law unto itself, rightly making its own demands that somehow set it beyond judgement as an ultimate, a sovereign good. Whilst admitting the social and personal significance of art, it is no part of my scheme to make children's interests subservient to those of art. Quite the reverse in fact. I want to exploit the educative power of the arts in the interests of the child's development – but this is not, I think, the same as to set an "instrumental" value upon art in the educational context. For my point about the instrumentalists is that by their own admission they seek to anatomize or adapt art to achieve educational goals that are neither art-based nor, necessarily, arts-related, whereas it is the *particular* quality of artistic experience that I am concerned with. It is the development of what I want to call the poetic dimension of being, of sensibility, that I seek. And my justification for doing so is that art, no matter how contested an area of philosophical debate, is unique in human experience as a way of knowing and as a way of being. It will, of course, be incumbent upon me to explain what I mean by that statement in the course of the ensuing argument. For the present perhaps I may simply be permitted to repeat the point I have been trying to establish: any account of the arts in education must see *the experience of art* as central and indeed as sufficient. It is this factor which will distinguish arts education not simply from the "academic" sciences and the humanities but also from, for example, the "applied" craft-design-technology, from psycha or socio-drama, and the hand-making of simple musical instruments.

I feel it is important to bid for a relatively purist position at the outset, not in order subsequently to be able to cry Heresy the more readily but, in fact, to serve as the basis of a rich and fruitfully varied practice. However I would expect even amidst richness and variety to discern a clear and coherent pattern of connections. From a single seed a flourishing root system, many branches, much blossom and a myriad leaves – but an oak for all that. And my impression at the moment when one studies the arts in education is of looking at one of those old-fashioned children's mix-and-match books: a bosun's body with grandma's legs and the head of a giraffe. Neither fish nor foul. Little wonder if those seeking to make sense of arts education, from the "outside" as it were, find it all very confusing. As we try to discover the priorities needed in arts education we shall seem to rule out not only some of the things arts teachers and their pupils now do, but some of the things many of them value and enjoy doing. However I believe it is as important not to claim too much for the arts and for education through the arts, as it is to stake a claim to what is absolutely essential. I really don't think it helps either "outsiders" or those who practice in arts education to produce a catalogue of aims and claims that seems to exhaust all known human needs and goods. Apart from any consideration of credibility such claims can usually be just as easily made of most other subjects in the curriculum, even perhaps be more legitimately so made of some of them. For one of the claims I shall want to make for the arts in education is that in a number of important respects they actually stand the rest of the curriculum on its head. Which is to say that the arts are distinguished as odd, and as bearing perhaps unfamiliar, even exotic educational fruit. The aesthetic curriculum is heartfelt and the case for an aesthetic education must rest in the end on its appeal to the heart. As Pascal said,

"Le coeur a ses raisons que la raison ne connaît point".

Acknowledgements

Anyone writing a book out of his working experience is bound to be deeply indebted to all those who have partnered that experience. Most of what follows has been the subject of hours of discussion and experimentation with different groups of students and my first debt of gratitude must be to all of them for the conviviality and stimulation of those encounters.

There are, of course, more particular debts to acknowledge. For several years I served on the Assessment of Performance Unit's Aesthetic Development Group and I learned a very great deal from my fellow members during that period. The matrix discussed in Chapter 12 is a refinement of the model developed in the course of that association. In the Preface to this volume I draw upon an article I originally wrote for the journal *Aspects* and I am grateful to the editors for allowing me to adapt it for my present purposes. Taking up Andrew Brighton's challenge was an important factor in motivating this essay. I am also deeply grateful to Peggy Blackburn for permission to quote in full her late husband's poem "Hallowed".

Many individuals have been of the greatest help to me. Sue Newall and Sylvia Ford have shared the trials of preparing the manuscript from illegible scribbles and inaudible tape recordings. Liz Frangescou worked round the clock to create the final, immaculate type-script. Anne Obermer and the Michael Marks Charitable Trust have continued to ensure a regular flow of funds to sustain the research work in arts education at Exeter University. Barbara Barratt at Pergamon Press has remained a constant support and encouragement.

My most immediate and personal debt is however to my wife Kicoula who has provided the "cover" without which such an undertaking – irrespective of its eventual success – would have been impossible. Her constancy, commitment and patient criticism have spurred and informed the work at every step – though, of course, I must accept ultimate responsibility for it. I would like to think it was in some measure worthy of her confidence.

Ashprington, Devon
1983

Contents

xvi   *Contents*

CHAPTER 1

The Threat to Arts Education

The need to give coherence and definition to the aesthetic area of education is urgent. Economic cut backs and political reactivism have put arts education under considerable threat – however, some of the responses to this present crisis among arts educators themselves have been seriously misguided. In particular two factions have emerged recently whose approaches need to be challenged: I characterize them as the "academics" and the "instrumentalists". The basis of their argument is that their particular emphasis will allow the integration of the arts into the mainstream of the curriculum. I want to suggest that this is entirely to misconstrue the singular contribution that the arts could make to a child's general education – that the arts are different and that therein lies their strength.

★ ★ ★ ★ ★

From the centre ground of the legitimate curriculum there seems to be something incorrigible, something irredeemable about the arts. I have personally spent some time documenting and lamenting the peripheral status of the arts in education. I have shown elsewhere (Ross, 1975) that every major educational report of the last fifty years or so has given the fullest moral support to the role of the arts in education and yet, despite such widespread official endorsement, the arts have continued to be widely regarded and resourced as an educational frill. Which has inevitably meant that at times of economic difficulty the arts subjects and arts teachers are always at risk.

More recently – and particularly since James Callaghan's famous Ruskin College speech – there have been strong materialist and politically reactionary forces at work in education. "Back to Basics!" has been the cry – by which is meant that children should be taught the so-called basic skills necessary to getting a job and to getting Britain back on the road to economic recovery. There have followed, the Great Debate aside, a steady flow of official pronouncements and consultative papers, the general tenor of which has been unequivocally functionalist. Timely research evidence seemed to lend weight to the mounting disillusion with and assault upon so-called progressive and humanistic educational practices with the result that the arts, far from

1

receiving the familiar lip-service of the past, have been given the shortest of possible shrift. Again, this is a theme I have written about already (Ross, 1981) so I shall go no further into it here. In the event there has been some mild relenting amongst the policy-makers: the "core curriculum" has not been as rigidly identified or as aggressively promoted as was originally feared and the arts have been left with something to fight for if, nevertheless, in an even more acutely parlous situation.

There has followed a concerted drive on "accountability". The DES is requiring of LEA's, and the LEA's of their schools, clear statements on aims, objectives and provision. Which has meant pressure all round: on non-arts as well as arts departments. If the arts weather the storm one is bound to feel it will be no thanks to the "accounts" emanating from their various spokesmen. I have had the opportunity of studying curriculum statements by teachers, schools and arts advisers, and have for the most part found them embarrassing if not downright shocking to read, in as much as they reveal all too clearly the deep confusion that befogs the minds of most arts educators when we have to give some kind of rational account of what we are trying to do and how we wish to go about it.

Alongside official efforts to rationalize the curriculum and to make everyone accountable we have seen the emergence of the Assessment of Performance Unit (APU). I say "we have seen" but, taken too literally, this would give a false impression for, as I write, the majority of teachers and student teachers are entirely oblivious of its existence. I have always sensed an element of tacit official complicity in the widespread general ignorance surrounding APU activities, but if you actually enquire at Elizabeth House you will have at least some of your questions answered. And it should at once be clear that the on-going investigation of assessment practices in education and, more particularly, the study of possible new procedures for ascertaining a national picture of competence levels are all of a piece with the current hard-nosed emphasis upon educational productivity. On the face of it the APU has approached its task on a broad front and with an open mind. The school curriculum has been presented in terms of a number of cross-curricular "lines of development" and groups of experts established either to move directly into exploratory monitoring in the schools or, in some cases, to provide some sort of evidence or appraisal concerning the possibility and desirability of the monitoring and assessment of specific lines. As one would expect there has been the stress upon the "basic" lines: language, maths and science. Work has been going on in other areas including the area of aesthetics – however, APU attitudes have here been harder to read and the abrupt winding up of the aesthetic group's work in the summer of 1981 and the delay over the publication of its report rather endorse the general picture I have been drawing of the marked lack of enthusiasm at the policy-making level for the arts as central to the debate on the balance and efficiency of the new school curriculum.

In such a cold climate it has clearly been of the utmost importance that arts people keep close together. Whilst it would be hard to say that arts educators have gone so far as to slough off their habitual easy-going cast of mind to rise as one to rail at a benighted Establishment, there has been protestation – and there have been heroic gestures. David Aspin for instance chose to devote his inaugural lecture as Professor of Philosophy of Education at King's College to the plight of the arts in education – a brave thing to do in an academic institution, at the best of times. And then there was the spectacular last stand of Neil Bally at Imperial College in November 1981 over the issue of part-time lecturers in colleges of art – which led, among other things, on the one hand to his own near bankruptcy and on the other to the formation of a national association of lecturers in art education. Nor were the perils of the present situation lost upon the Gulbenkian Foundation, who, after three years work under the chairmanship of the UK director Peter Brinson, discharged a broadside of its own: *The Arts in Schools* (1982). This Report presents the case for the arts in education in an astringently written and carefully structured argument and in its way it fills an awkward and embarrassing gap in the political literature. It is for the most part very readable and offers an intelligible and authoritative over-view of what arts educators are doing and of why the arts offer children unique opportunities for learning. If one has a reservation it is not so much about the quality of the Report itself as about the thinking that instituted it. It was conceived by the Foundation as contributing to educational policy making at the highest level – as a kind of ready-reckoner or perhaps primer for administrators and executives with no special knowledge of the arts yet reasonably disposed to do the right thing by them.

Whilst I remain rather doubtful about the actual impact upon official thinking and decision making of any of the above initiatives, I believe they will have in fact made important contributions, all three, to the morale and performance of arts educators. The Gulbenkian Report recommends the setting up of a National Council for Arts Education and such an outcome alone would be sufficient vindication of the group's work. They are significant demonstrations of commitment and conviction, and at the very least will have stayed the hand of the trimmer in lending authority and some passion to grass-roots resistance. But for me the real issue lies elsewhere. I don't deny it is important to shout, to wave the flag, even to try and have a sensible word in the top man's ear. The resistance clearly has to be vigorous and on as broad a front as we can make it not least because, once axed, arts courses and arts teachers can make no impact at all. And perhaps the actual threat to jobs and courses is as real as many people fear (take for instance the

UGC's unparalleled blitz upon drama and music departments in its recommended restructuring of universities). In hard economic times expediency
rules and some authorities and institutions pick off the softest targets instead
of facing the much more difficult consequences of defending their overall
conception of a suitable education package and distributing the consequences
of contraction equally across the board.

When the worst of the storm has passed we may find, perhaps surprisingly,
much of what we value in arts education has gone for good. Whatever
happens, however, we shall not have fallen victim to a pack of Philistines
hell-bent on our destruction. The arts may always have been misunderstood
and seriously neglected and ignored in education, but there are few people
committed to seeing the arts in education go down. You don't find
councillors, governors, CEO's or Head Teachers – by and large – leading an
anti-arts lobby. The fact of the matter is more often the reverse: amongst the
powers-that-be you are much more likely to find a benign if uncomprehending acquiescence in all things artistic and to all things cultural. 'Not very
knowledgeable myself I'm afraid'. Apologetic rather than apoplectic. And,
on those rare occasions when the arts person *is* faced with resolute opposition
– informed or otherwise – one has to wonder whether the kinds of arguments
propounded in the Gulbenkian Report would really make much of a defence.
The report, sponsored as it was, is surely likely to appear as special pleading
on behalf of an interested party. But, as I have said, for me the issue is rather
different. If the current attempt to smother the arts is the result neither of
ignorance nor malice in high places but, rather, merely an expedient device
for resolving an excruciating administrative problem, what can we make of
the incontestable fact that, for whatever reason, the arts have always
struggled and must presumably go on struggling to retain some sort of
presence upon the educational scene? However, the present political bosses
seem to have no conception of the cultural consequences of failing to provide
for the aesthetic dimension in education.

What of the incorrigible and irredeemable character of arts education? Is
such indeed the case? And if so, why? Is there something incorrigible and
irredeemable about art itself? I personally think there is and shall be coming
to that. The "instrumentalist" faction in arts education is, I think, very
sensible of these characteristics, though they might not be aware of the sway
they hold over their own conscious decisions, for the instrumentalist seeks to
bring the arts into line with the tendency of the traditional curriculum in the
belief that since we'll never beat them we had better join them. Not, of
course, in order to surrender your basic principles but as a way of securing at
least some undisputed ground upon which to raise and realize the educational
potential of the arts. The traditional school curriculum has always been
committed in the simplest and most straightforward terms to a programme of
accelerated socialization: its criteria are uncomplicatedly academic and

pragmatic. Schooling is to teach children to be useful and effective in the world. This means that they will learn – and must demonstrate that they have learned – skills of practical value, and also have acquired knowledge to support such skills. That's what James Callaghan was interested to remind us. They may, as Mary Warnock (in Ross, 1983) advocates, be further brought to associate such learning with "pleasure", may come to see, as she suggests, that power (over oneself, over the world of objects, even over other people sometimes) is the source of all real pleasure and that the ultimate reward of schooling is the pleasure that power gives.

Of course schools are not so barefaced in their pursuit of the pragmatic, of what David Jones (1959) has called the "utile", as to insist upon unrelieved Gradgrind: "Facts, facts, facts". Most schools acknowledge, alongside the aesthetic, children's social, personal and moral needs. But, I suggest, even here, there is a clear connection drawn between learning and socially acceptable forms of educational productivity: the disabling or inhibiting effects of bad feeling and short-sightedness, arising from whatever source, are recognized by the system as threatening to the accounting process that is the basis of all good school management and so as meriting at least some official attention. But this is a notably controversial area where schools are more than likely to feel that they're on a hiding to nothing whatever they do. If they get too close to the child they're accused of infringing privacy and undermining parental authority; if they keep a respectful distance then when something does go wrong (but never when it goes right) there will be general recriminations and scapegoating all round. The APU was as uncomfortable with its Social and Moral Development Project as the proverbial cat on the hot tin roof.

The arts educator who embraces neither the academic nor the instrumental cause faces a very acute problem of legitimacy; much more acute, for example, than that of the school counsellor, the RE teacher or the careers adviser, all of whom have their own problems of credibility. Required to account for himself in terms of a school's productivity he may be forced to rationalize very much along the lines taken by the Gulbenkian writers, and to lay out a ground plan that covers everything from intelligence to manipulative dexterity taking in a fair number of socially acceptable attitudes and values on the way. Whereas what he wants to say, probably, is that he has been trained as an artist – which will certainly be so unless his qualifications are in English in which case he may have some claim to being a critic – that art has been and remains vital to his way of life, and that, somehow, he wants to involve children in his own enthusiasm. He may further volunteer that his interest in art has made his own life and career somewhat problematic and that he wouldn't find it easy either to talk about his own creative work or to say why certain works of other artists are of enduring importance to him. He'd probably prefer not to have to go into all that but to be allowed to go on

teaching what he feels he knows and sharing what he feels to be important –
with no questions asked. And the galling thing is that until relatively recently
the matter would in all probability have been allowed to rest there.
Prospective art teachers, for instance would attend for interview with a
portfolio of their work (and if already teaching, some of their children's
work), would be assessed on artistic grounds (largely if not solely) and trusted
to get on with essentially artistic work once appointed. Musicians were
usually asked to audition, and drama candidates have been asked to conduct
group improvisations (no English teacher that I ever heard of has been asked
to submit his own writing or read from his own poetry, but then English, as
traditionally conceived and taught is certainly not an arts subject (see Ross,
1975). Something I would join Peter Abbs (1981) in strongly wishing to see
altered.)

What I am saying is that there was a time, whatever arts teachers made of
it, when they were assumed to be artists teaching the arts and when such an
assumption needed no apology. That this is no longer the case provides
simultaneously the occasion for an assessment of that assumption, together
with its implications for education, and for the kind of desperate clutching
after straws that I have just been instancing. In other words I see great
advantage in challenging the assumption that every arts teacher is an artist
and that what he teaches is art while recognizing that faced with the novel and
uncongenial task of finding unfamiliar words for familiar experience, the arts
teacher may lose credibility in being forced to give a predictably inadequate
account of himself. It is in such a climate that the blandishments of the
instrumentalists and the academicists seem so attractive and it is to offer an
alternative account securely tied to the legitimacy of art itself that this essay is
committed.

Discussion about the purpose of arts education need not be frustrated by
the controversy that has traditionally surrounded discussions about art and
aesthetics. We can simply choose to place the experience of art at the heart of
the aesthetic curriculum, may confidently declare the experience of art to be a
sufficient cause for arts education and repudiate alternative suggestions that,
for instance, general creativity, manipulative or social skills acquired in the
course of arts-associated activity (such as role-play or graphic design or group
work) are somehow more legitimate, more defensible. But, naturally, we
would only feel able to make this claim if we were personally convinced of the
intrinsic value of art in human experience. And, if we were prepared to
accept – and defend – the contentious condition of art itself. We would be
saying in effect, there's nothing contentious about the basis and scope of our
work as educators, however the area of human experience that we are
concerned with is every bit as fluid, as problematic, as subject to contention
and confusion as the fields of history, science and mathematics. (That line
might raise an eyebrow or two.) We share with our other arts colleagues an

enduring interest in the phenomenon of art – in the incessant process of revaluation that has been the history of art since time immemorial. Our work is a tentative formulation as to the present significance of art, informed by our first-hand experience and the most recent "research" we have been able to assimilate. Which means that we must expect arts teachers to remain aesthetically active in their own right.

But I have already more than hinted that the arts are not merely intrinsically contentious as perhaps are all areas of human enquiry, they are placed, by society at large, in a somewhat special category with respect to normal, every-day, pragmatic goings-on. The arts and artists – even when not behaving in a strikingly depraved or abhorrent fashion – are odd, unsafe, frivolous, threatening, wasteful, disruptive: all those things that are at odds with the business of sensibly getting on with making a living, making war, maintaining the status quo. Of course the history of art provides adequate evidence of the public-spiritedness and serviceability of the arts, as sustaining and enlivening social and religious life, as providing useful and tradable artifacts, as crystallizing and anticipating revelations of the spirit and of the imagination. But the record also shows the artist – frequently identified with magic or sorcery – is a somewhat unreliable servant, owing allegiance to other worlds, to other value-systems. A powerful ally, and formidable adversary. Not to be bought since in selling himself he somehow abrogates his powers. Frequently protected by taboo. Sacrosanct. It is not a little astonishing that in a time when, apparently, the mass of people are totally uninterested in and even unaware of the issues that animate the art world, acts of violence by ordinary people against works of art (as if somehow they were more of a threat than the artist who made them) are still regularly reported. If society has a love-hate relationship with art (as it doesn't seem on the whole to have with medicine or engineering or animal husbandry for instance) it is hardly surprising that general attitudes to arts education are at least ambivalent and, that being the case, that arts teachers have to adjust to living dangerously on a switch-back of public opinion, such as to mark them off almost completely from their non-arts colleagues. One can only conclude that arts teachers *are* different.

We should in my view endeavour to remain so. That is the point I want to make. Not that we should make the kinds of conforming adjustments that are being wished upon us and in many quarters granted, but rather that we should clarify our understanding of what is *special* about arts education the more confidently to defend its frontiers. It sounds a rather primitive, not to say reactionary attitude – all this beating of the bounds – but I would argue we shall never be in a position to go beyond our own frontier (to link up, for instance, with other subjects) until, in a sense, we have secured it. And within arts education, the work is largely yet to do: and what is worse the territory is even now being sold off piecemeal to the speculators by our own people. This of course is the point at which we are, to some extent, on our own. This is where we have to say what we mean by art, by the experience of art, where we establish the co-ordinates of our own position in the contested field. And no individual teacher can avoid doing so. My account, which now follows, will be true of my own experience. I think a good deal of it could be corroborated by the evidence of others so I can advance my case with some confidence, but never I hope dogmatically, since the fine print of even my own views is shifting all the time anyway. It is unlikely that any one account of art will correlate entirely with another. What matters is not so much that we should agree in every detail as that our ideas and actions should be subject to objective evaluation and that we ourselves should be capable of such objectivity in evaluating our own actions and ideas. Then the consensus we absolutely must have will become at least a possibility: a consensus that would not be constraining upon individual action but rather the opposite, freeing within a pervasive concordance.

CHAPTER 2

Art, a Way of Knowing

Drawing upon the notions of the "potential space" (Winnicott) and the "boundary" (Leach) I propose a view of art as at odds with the mundane, secular, pragmatic concerns of everyday. Art is committed to the ordering of individual and social values, to promoting intelligent feeling, to the continual processes of self-renewal and self-regeneration so vital to the sense we have of life as having personal meaning for us. Art is a way of seeing, rather than a particular class of objects – to see "artistically" means treating "designs" (sensuous forms) as signs and the world as numinous or sacred. The basis of such seeing is human sensibility.

*   *   *   *   *

In support of my thesis that the arts are different, and of the corollary that if arts education is truly to reflect the spirit of art it too must accept odd-ball, even outsider status (though never a merely peripheral role) I want to draw together two ideas from writers who seem to me to have a great deal to offer the arts in education. I have already worked out in some detail what I take to be the implications for arts education of some of D.W. Winnicott's ideas (Ross, 1978). In particular I have found his concepts of the "potential space" and the "transitional object" (Winnicott, 1971) provocative of much fruitful thinking. Winnicott is offering a conceptual model to help us think about the critically important relationship between mother and infant in the early stages of "playing". He proposes an area of overlap between the subjectivity of the mother and the subjectivity of the child within which gratuitously pleasurable activities can take place. Play is born of the spontaneous drive to explore, investigate, manipulate, alter and, above all, order. The making or discovery of order – and so of what is enduring - is the impulse, so Winnicott suggests, that fuels all our creative acts. I shall want to suggest in my own way that that impulse is quintessentially *aesthetic*. It will be remembered that he goes on to insist that all healthy and reasonably well-adjusted people live creatively by simple virtue of their incessant and restless seeking after pattern, order and meaning in the world. The so-called "potential space" is a privileged area of social interaction between mother and child in which the

child, under the protective care and cover – and in the proferred emotional
milieu – of the mother, begins to establish the object world as amenable to
manipulation: as meaningful and as desirable.

Winnicott insists that the spirit of playfulness is all-important in this
process of "worlding" the child, making the point that unless the mother can
play with the child, can be playful herself, there can be no healthy
development of the child in the cultural field. Fortunately nature gives most
parents adequate resources for this vital task: we don't have to be super-
mums and super-dads, although we must be "good-enough".

Winnicott gives us therefore the idea of play, creativity and culture
generally developing within a protective and special "area" that is somehow
sacred to the non-pragmatic dimension of experience. The anthropologist,
Edmund Leach, my second source, writing from a very different viewpoint,
though not one entirely unrelated to the notion of cultural development,
namely the area of myth and religious ritual, also proposes a model that
provides for a sacred area, a space set apart from the routine, the useful
means-to-ends related activities of everyday human transaction. He draws
our attention (Leach 1976) to the special characteristics of the "boundary":

> "A boundary separates two zones of social space-time which are *normal,
> time-bound, clear-cut, central, secular*, but the spacial and temporal markers which
> actually serve as boundaries are themselves *abnormal, timeless, ambiguous, at the
> edge, sacred*." (Page 35)

Reading this passage for the first time I was startled by the precise fit, as I saw
it, between this account of the boundary type characteristics of myth and
religious ritual, and the traditional and continuing circumstances surrounding art. And, of course, not simply art but all those various experiences of the
"poetic" in reverie and daydream that seem to deny, or at least conflict with,
the values of common-sense, everyday practicality. One might easily go
further and suggest that the artist-shaman figure in the tribal setting and the
avant-garde in our own culture share at least this condition of being suspect –
or, to use another word which Leach applies to the boundary – "taboo". I
won't develop the argument further, for the connection between art and the
abnormal, timeless, ambiguous, at the edge, sacred, is I think sufficiently
uncontroversial to need no further instancing. And the correspondence
with Winnicott's "potential space" is sufficiently close for us to conjecture at
least a very close identification between the two. They are in their different
ways proposing the crucible in which culture is generated: Winnicott in
terms of the life of the individual, Leach in terms of the life of a people.

Leach goes on to write about the special character of Sunday – a
"boundary" day marking off one working (secular) week from another. It is
in "no time", nothing "normal" or "central" happens – indeed it is, or used to
be, prohibited from so happening. Sunday, on the other hand, is not merely a
negative time/space: it is the day for ritual renewal, for personal re-

consecration and recreation. It is of course, holy – literally devoted to what is hale or health giving. It is sacred. Sunday is the day for communion with and is dedicated to the values of what Leach call "the Other World": the boundary.

> "The concept of the Other World is generated by direct inversion of the characteristics of ordinary experience. This World is inhabited by mortal, impotent men, who live out their lives in normal time in which events happen in sequence, one after the other. In this world we get older and older 'all the time' and in the end we die. The Other World is inhabited by immortal, omnipotent gods, who exist perpetually in abnormal time in which past, present and future all co-exist 'simultaneously'. (Page 81)

The reader who has followed me thus far will now see why I find Leach both illuminating and re-assuring. I have referred to the incorrigible and irredeemable description that arts education traditionally attracts. I have argued that art is "different" and, by implication, that arts education (and arts educators) are also "different". The problem is of course that this apparently inescapable fact which I have now accounted for in Leach's terms of being different, being odd-ball, being outsider, has meant almost inevitably, being cast out. Being placed at the edge of things. Betwixt and between: liminal. This raises a crucial question for arts education. If we are, by definition almost, beyond the pale of normal, central, secular life – and the school seems dedicated unequivocally to a secular set of values – must we simply resign ourselves to having to operate on the edge of things, to being at best tolerated and at the worst an expendable irrelevance? What chance have we of a place, what reason is there in arguing for a place at the centre of things, or to use current parlance, at the "core"? If privation, discomfiture and hardship are to be the price of sticking to the idea of art in arts education should we not perhaps either relinquish it (I have already suggested this is now a fairly popular view) or move out altogether and operate wholly on an extra-curricular basis?

I think we can certainly see why many of the most exciting arts experiences currently on offer to children and young people do, in fact, take place after school and out of school. In the evenings, at weekends, in the holidays, in art centres, dance centres, drama centres, music centres and the like. And when confronted with the farcical situations which obtain in many schools (drama in the dining hall, music in the corridor) one has very seriously to wonder whether more harm than good were being done by "school" arts. If you are looking for an arrangement that respects art as "timeless", "ambiguous" and "sacred" you should perhaps not be too surprised to find schools somewhat uncongenial places. Yet very few of us, I suspect, are ready yet to accept that such a situation is inevitable; to settle for strategic withdrawal even should a professionally satisfactory arrangement be worked out (e.g. art teachers employed to work in art centres). For to abandon schooling to the absolute and undisputed sway of Mammon and all that would entail would be to sacrifice education on the altar of opportunism – to settle for the simpler concept of "training". And, as far as I know, no one either within or outside the arts is yet prepared to go quite that far though one might be forgiven, perhaps, for thinking that that more or less represents the spirit of such documents as *"The School Curriculum"*. (1981)

The concept of education as induction into the good life, life abundant, is not simply a romantic white whale, born of a misty liberalism and destined to beach itself upon the sands of a dried out labour market. Schools are, it goes without saying, bound to be committed to the preparation of children for such work as there might be. But they are also equally bound to provide children with such other resources as they will need to make sense of life, in particular of their own lives, to form sustaining relationships with other people, to continue their education throughout life, to the finding of meaning and value in the world. Perhaps above all to develop the roots of a healthy motivational system. Such a task is of course infinitely more onerous than mere training. It is however *the* task to which the teacher has traditionally been called. And arguably the one that most attracts young people into teaching in the first place. I am fairly confident however it is an aspect of teaching still little understood and almost wholly unconsidered in the preparation of the student teacher. Just as it is easier to teach the skills of medium control in the arts than it is to teach the skills of creativity, perception and of composition, so it is easier to transfer educational freight from teacher to learner than it is to release the springs of self-motivation that bring in the prospect of personal knowledge.

I want it to be quite clear that I am not talking about "therapy" here, any more than I have in mind the good works of the school counsellor. I am speaking of the attitudes and practices of all teachers in their everyday encounters with all children. Of their practice, their methods, the messages transmitted by the so-called "hidden" (though in practice all too manifest) curriculum. Winnicott saw the "potential space" as the site of all cultural and intellectual activities, so there has to be a sense in which all education, whether in science or history or language or art, needs to be imbued with the spirit of play and, at least on occasion, imbued with the values of Leach's Other World. Creativity, intuition, imagination and feeling are not, or should not be, the prerogative of the arts. Therapy, it seems to me, is for people who, for some reason, have become bogged down, blocked or trapped in psychic quicksand. Whose progress is seriously impeded and who are therefore in need of rescue by a specialist: a therapist. The commitment to expression, creativity and imagination in education is simply the commitment to the principle of life-abundance – and *all* teachers have to be, as a qualification for their work, committed to that principle and expert in its practice. And life-abundance is quintessentially the aesthetic principle embodied as "the art of living".

The arts belong to the mainstream of education on both sacred and secular grounds. Not only in the sense that they can be deployed for secular ends or that arts education can have its own practical or vocational outcomes, but also, of course, in the sense that for all their alleged other-worldliness the arts are rooted in everyday experience and depend upon sensory perception and material media for their enactment. It is always salutary to think of the arts curriculum and the whole curriculum as a continuum and not in terms of sacred and secular poles. Unfortunately the schism is deeply drawn with the result that the bulk of the curriculum seems to have become unrelentingly secular and pragmatic in emphasis and, so, bound to the productivity ethos and regulated by industrial style management practices, while for their part the arts are openly coerced either into similar or servicing roles. Where they choose to stay out of step the arts may suffer routine relegation to obscurity. It is worth noting in passing that those arts teachers who have decided that the best way to legitimatize their work is to have it examined, just like all the other subjects in the curriculum, have been counting the costs in terms of some considerable sacrifice in autonomy not to say integrity for what turn out in practice to be the often illusory benefits of certification. Arts successes at CSE and GCE carry very little weight either with employers or in higher education. It seems you just cannot win if you are an arts person. You might try changing your spots but you do not actually fool anyone. I don't like to see the arts perched at the sacred end of the curriculum see-saw, committed to some sort of a thankless balancing act. As I say, the curriculum needs to be conceived as a whole – with sacred and secular concerns inextricably intertwined and not parcelled out as the defining responsibilities of particular factions. Education as a whole is an initiation, a rite of passage. Nevertheless for all that one might wish to argue for the sacredness of the sciences and the proper secularity of the arts there is a sense in which the arts are by definition "liminal", consecrated to and witness of the "other world". This characteristic ambivalence arises from the nature of artistic experience and artistic meaning, resting essentially on the mediation of "poetic" truth. Now the last thing one wants at this point of the discussion is to start introducing mystifying terms – and with all this talk of the sacred and of other worlds there has probably been too much of that already. But art seeks the truth by visionary means (by synthesis rather than analysis) whether it be truth about the world without or the world within. Its practice is neither logical nor empirical though it has to be in the strictest sense rational since all intelligent behaviour is grounded in mind.

But it is mind operating upon the basis of feeling: if art has a characteristic mode of mental operation then the only word we have for it, no matter how unsatisfactory, is the word "sensibility" – which the Shorter Oxford Dictionary defines as "the power or faculty of feeling". Art arises in virtue of sensibility and returns to nourish it by means of its objects: sacred objects imbued with revelatory power. The power of revelation ("anagnorisis") inheres in all matter subjected to imaginative perception and this is the "fact" that underlies the whole of man's artistic practice. Material phenomena as we shall see have a sacramental or numinous aspect: all sensuous forms necessarily "speak", directly, without recourse to concepts or words. The old, earthenware jug on my sideboard at home, seems to speak of fullness, plenitude, assurance, tranquillity. It is not symbolic in the sense that it "refers" to those ideas or stands somehow in lieu of them. Rather, as Louis Arnaud Reid suggests, that they are the "meaning embodied" in its materiality, or, in the words of Robert Plant Armstrong (1975), this is the nature of its "affecting presence". We come to know aesthetically directly, by encountering the world not through other people's descriptions, but "face to face". We read art as we read persons, essentially with intelligent sensing. I would say, with sensibility. No one would want to deny sensibility to the practice of the sciences and humanities, but those investigations are conducted largely in other terms and exploit man's capacity for rationality and logic. They may, with the arts, equally address psychological as material or sociological problems but they do so, essentially, from the standpoint of reason where the arts exploit the mind's intuitive powers. Mind as feeling, that is. And the way of the "power or faculty of feeling" is the way of the abnormal, the timeless, the ambiguous, the borderline, the sacred. Which is why the arts are both irretrievably "other" with respect to the normal, the time-bound, the clear-cut, the central, the secular, and why at least in some essential respects, the arts curriculum, to adapt Leach's words, has to be generated by direct inversion of the characteristics of the ordinary curriculum.

All of which perhaps seems like giving up any claim to legitimacy that might still remain to the arts, the abandoning of any hope we might have had of securing a seat at the curriculum table. But I think not so. I am convinced that it is only by building our practice on some such premise as the above that we have any chance of appearing, let alone feeling, authentic – and I sense that those we are from time to time compelled to address and whose authorization we need are half-persuaded already that, as centaurs rather than work-horses, we are likely to make unusual demands and raise awkward problems.

In other words we are understood as approaching the world from the poetic end of things: all that remains is to demonstrate that we are properly equipped to work in this way and that the children we teach are gaining poetic access to truths they value and that are of some objective significance. If the management actually does still need persuading – if it still needs its ear bent with well-modulated argument, such argument must first have been well-rehearsed *within* (even if it cannot be entirely confined to) the arts fraternity.

Here, clarity of mind is needed to give credence to matter both of thought and practice. The management, I feel certain, is ready to trust the arts people to know what they are doing and what they do best. Even to make their own claims concerning what is valuable, what is successful and what is not. This essay is addressed to the arts education fraternity on the assumption that the weakness of arts education lies in the failure to make our work tell, and only to management in so far as management needs to take an interest in the internal matters of a particular branch of the profession. Management is most likely to be impressed by "results" anyway. We must be able to make our case, and if required to do so, not on idealogical or theoretical grounds – which I regard are largely internal matters – but as demonstrated in outcomes.

I do not deny that there might be a case for underlining from time to time what we feel actually count as the legitimate outcomes of arts education. But we are completely barking up the wrong tree if we think our salvation lies either in coming up with the right sounding arguments or the right kind of examination results. It lies rather in re-awakening people's own commitment to and engagement in the "other" world, the need of poetic mediation, and we do so best by giving them, through the work of the children we teach, occasions for such experience, here and now, there and then. This essay will not then argue a case for the significance of art in human experience. I shall assume that the people to whom it is principally addressed are already persuaded – and that those to whom they are responsible need simply to be reminded, in John Blacking's words, that history sufficiently demonstrates the inherently artistic nature of man. I shall rather proceed with the business of trying to sort out the principles upon which right practice in arts education might be based. If the arts are facing a crisis in education, and I believe that at least in some respects they are, it may be not so much because our credentials are in question as that we have failed politically.

Before going on to do so, I just want to consider for a moment what objection might be raised against this commitment to "difference", to "otherness". I have already tried to rebut allegations of romantic bias. Perhaps not wholly successfully. I must grant that my personal debt is to those artists, poets, musicians who have, through their art, enriched my life, and whose art now seems to be an important constituent of the person I feel myself to be. Though I am necessarily thinking in the first place of individuals, finding and communicating their personal visions, I am not thinking of art as aggravation, although I would want to argue that there is a sense in which all art is inherently just that. For me any account of the arts in education has to begin with the experience and education of the individual and I would very much agree with Herbert Marcuse (1979) that the revolutionary character of art has to operate upon each one of us individually before it can be seen as a liberating principle at work within society as a whole. I am, of course, apprehensive of writing about the Other World and the sacred lest my argument be dismissed as an appeal to religious or mystical experience. But I cannot fudge the matter and disclaim the centrality for me of the notion of the "numinous" in art. For the reason already given that sensuous forms signify of themselves, that pursuit of "poetic" meaning is what activates artistic perception. And such meaning, if it is not in itself divine, is at least, divined, revealed, given – like grace.

I am of course speaking here neither of the subject matter nor of the particular impact of individual works of art. Nor am I suggesting that the only valid achievement in art is the celebration of the sublime and of the transcendental. Art, of course, covers every possible human experience, and must encompass death as well as life, pain as much as pleasure – may be made at the behest of an overlord, to delight a child, in moments of idleness, to relieve the tedium of alienating labour, to stir us to action. But all those different manifestations of what we call art nevertheless comply with my basic premise that art is a particular way of knowing. I have chosen to call it "poetic". An art object is always an artifact made or selected to be used "poetically" – i.e. with an eye to the evocative, the emotional power of its design. Joseph Margolis (1980) has given the following austere definition of a work of art.

"A work of art is an artifact considered with respect to its design". (Page 89)

On the face of it this seems a pretty bald and unpromising account, and yet, if we allow the notion of design to take in the affective dimension – and nothing he says suggests we should not – then his definition has the great value of pointing us directly at the key feature of aesthetic discourse. It also neatly rules out any dichotomy between form and content; if art has a message it is embodied in the very fact of its design – its "dessein".

I would remind those who argue for a more secular, more functionalist view of arts education, that art itself can be as socially disturbing and as challenging as any political slogan, treatise or documentary. Probably infinitely more so. I simply want to preserve the distinction and in so doing to "reserve" the potential space, the boundary zone of poetic vision and poetic apprehension. To those who might see me as advocating a dangerously isolationist policy that could only in the end rebound upon us with even more disastrous consequences, I say that there is no point in courting respectability by trying to play the academic stock market. That line has surely already been shown as the sell out it is. Giving Caesar his due may be just common sense, but allowing academic criteria to dominate the arts curriculum is a certain way of losing credibility with the very people the curriculum is designed to serve: the students.

I do not for a moment disparage either the academic study of the arts or the development in children of the practical skills required for successful artistic application. However, for me at least, both these elements must be subordinate to the cultural role of the arts as personally and socially re-generative. And within the tri-partite school curriculum already referred to, I see the arts as primarily committed to the child's cultural development. If, as I believe, art is a way of knowing, a medium of human understanding *in its own right*, then there can be no more urgent a task for arts educators than to initiate their pupils as artists and as users of the arts.

CHAPTER 3

Sensibility

Sensibility is a vital faculty affecting the quality and effectiveness of everyone's life – it is not merely the distinguishing characteristic of the cultured classes or of artists. The faculty of feeling is responsible for the basic ability to distinguish formal coherence in the world: through appropriate experience the scope and quality of sensibility may be enhanced and the individual's quality of experience hugely enriched. In particular aesthetic perception finds significance intrinsic to the phenomena of experience, values things in themselves. Works of art are objects perceived as being not only of intrinsic interest but as embodying poetic meaning.

★　★　★　★　★

"Sensibility" is neither a popular nor a fashionable word – but then nor is "aesthetic". Yet I believe we must try to re-establish both of them in education despite the observation of Raymond Williams (1976), speaking of sensibility, that the word has in recent years faded from active discussion. "It is significant", he writes, "that in its actual range (which is what is fundamentally at issue) no adequate replacement has been found". In his account of the word's development, Williams points out first of all its fundamental association with the notions of sense, sensation and sensuous perception. He then goes on to note Sterne's use of the word in 1768. Basically sensibility means *the ability to feel*. During the nineteenth century it became increasingly associated with aesthetic and artistic experience. The word found considerable favour in writings about aesthetics in the first half of the twentieth century and

> "for an important period, sensibility was that from which art proceeded and through which it was received". (Williams, 1976, Page 238)

I am not competent to account for its demise since that time; however I wonder whether this increased specialization in its application to the arts, and what is more, its association with a particular period of art criticism, the so-called New Criticism of the 20's and 30's, did not have something to do with it. The New Criticism of those days is now under direct attack in, for example, literary circles, and the structuralists, fighting an establishment raised upon the principles embodied in that earlier movement, are unlikely to find any use for a word so suggestive of everything they are concerned to overthrow.

In invoking this word "sensibility" then I am clearly going to be in difficulty since there can be few more profitless tasks (as the experience of any linguistic conservationist will testify) than to row against the tide of usage, particularly when it is in flood. One looks in vain for any sign of the word sensibility in current philosophical and critical discourse in aesthetics. Furthermore, its traditional association with High Art and Polite Society makes it possibly an even more bizarre choice for someone seeking to institute a populist base for education through the arts. And yet, as Williams has said, there is no adequate alternative. My excuse must be that we absolutely have to speak of the faculty of feeling if we are to discuss the role of the arts, or the aesthetic principle, in education. No other word that I know of offers as encapsulating a definition of what we mean when we speak of the appraisal of aesthetic experience. I am hoping that by saying reasonably clearly how I intend using it I may escape being either dismissed as wilfully reactionary or misunderstood as embodying a system of values and attitudes quite foreign to the thrust of my argument. I want to turn the clock well back to those words of Sterne (quoted by Williams, Page 237) and root my usage in the sense of "the ability to feel":

"dear Sensibility! source ... unexhausted of all that's precious in our joys, or costly in our sorrows."

We must prise the word sensibility, like the word aesthetic, apart from its somewhat exclusive, though relatively recent historical association with a particular movement in art. We want sensibility like aesthetics to stand for the "formative" faculty of human mind and not simply that particular manifestation of the aesthetic in art, still less High Art. But only in the end to come back to art and recognize sensibility as the faculty of mind, the mental activity, which gives access to the impact and meaning of art. Sensibility proclaims feeling as a function of intelligence: as a way of knowing, as a means to understanding.

We may discern sensibility at work whenever we seek coherence in mental information. Sensibility is that mode of mental operation that responds to clues and reaches out to grasp or apprehend the structural principle governing the integration of raw inchoate information into shapes, patterns and forms that "conform" with our feeling for particular coherences. We may well wonder about the origins of our sense of order and the literature on the subject is very considerable (for example see Gombrich, 1980). My own inclination is to side with those who see perception as the projection of mind upon matter and who choose to interpret our intuitive ability to distinguish only an apparently narrow range of structures in the material environment as indicating the limited circuitry available for mental operations in the brain. These purely physical or environmental structures have their counterparts in the world of abstract and symbolic thought. Polanyi and Prosch (1976) in their illuminating account of the act of creation, see sensibility as comprising two interacting processes: intuition and imagination. They stress the importance of imagination as the formative faculty of the mind interpreting the perceptual or conceptual clues available to it in an urgent and ceaseless quest for structure and hence for meaning. Imagination they say does not work like a computer, searching every possible, and mostly useless alternative. Imagination works by leaping towards a solution, producing ideas or hypotheses "that are guided by a fine sense of their plausibility, ideas which contain aspects of the solution from the start". The sequence of events goes something like this:

> "First an idea appears given by intuition to be pondered by imagination. Second, the imagination is let loose to ferret out a path of possible clues, guided by intuitive feelings. And third, an idea offers itself intuitively as a possible conclusion, to be pondered in its turn in the light of the imagination." (Polanyi and Prosch, 1976)

My use of the word "sensibility" would cover this activity in all the realms of mental forming, which makes every search for form an aesthetic operation. This is, it seems to me, very much what happens when we try to make sense of either subjective or objective phenomena: the heart of the process is the deep guidance-system that Polanyi and Prosch call "intutitive feeling". It is essentially *our intuitive feeling for structural possibility* and that is what I mean by sensibility. Imagination, however, does the donkey-work of problem solving, but informed always by this quality of mental divination whereby the solution is in some sense anticipated before the work of problem solving has begun. It seems to me what intuitive feeling does is to identify the problem or to supply the structural principle in terms of which the problematic material might be integrated. Without such a formulation or possible structure, no work on the problem is possible. There are innumerable instances of creative work in the sciences as well as in the arts proceeding precisely upon these lines – i.e. as imagination working upon the intuitive divinations of sensibility. However, we shall want to make a further claim for what Witkin (1974) has called the *intelligence of feeling*: namely that it is especially suited to the solving of sensate (as distinct from conceptual) problems: which is to say that we use imagination infused with our intuitive feeling for form, particularly in the realization of new *feeling forms*. The point may again be supported by reference to Polanyi and Prosch. They make a careful distinction between the way we attend to conceptual symbols and the way we attend to percepts. In the normal use of language, the words we use (the subsidiaries in information processing) have no *intrinsic interest* (ii) for us. We focus our attention rather on what they refer to: not on the words as such, but rather on the meaning they carry. The authors diagram this process thus

(−ii)   (+ii)
subsidiaries   ——————————————▶   focus

With works of art however and all objects aesthetically appraised we take intrinsic interest in the subsidiaries so called, in the sensuous qualities of the artifact. For, as Louis Arnaud Reid has said, art functions as "meaning embodied".

(+ii)   ——————————————▶   (+ii)

embodiment   ◀——————————————   meaning

Since it is the function of sensibility to discover form – where form itself embodies meaning rather than referring to or conveying it – we might expect the disclosing of such embodied meaning to be the business of sensibility – of the intelligence of feeling. To achieve meaning, information requires stabilizing as structure, and structure is coherence or design (whether of concord or discord). A coherent design is one in which a structural principle is evidently at work. It might be the principle of balance or of counterpoint; perhaps of repetition or of echo (reciprocation). In making sense of a design we are on the look out for clues as to its structural principle. The Eysenck test of Visual Aesthetic Sensitivity is devised to see whether the participants can "abstract" the structural principle at work in the paired designs and, having done so, appreciate the coherence of the one design as against the relative incoherence of its partner. It is a fair test of visual aesthetic sensitivity if you accept Eysenck's criteria of sensuous coherence: and therein lies the problem. No attempt is made in the test either to ascertain the participants' responses to the expressive character of the designs or indeed to see whether they can identify the organizing concept serving as the principle of a particular coherence. Some would argue that such an omission seriously undermines the test's claim as discriminating aesthetic sensitivity (which Eysenck goes so far as to equate with "good taste" and the feeling for beauty), since it reduces aesthetic perception to an elementary – one might also say to a trivial – level.

This principle of coherence is very important in aesthetics for, as I have argued, it is the basis of all aesthetic judgements. I think we may reasonably take the view that when we talk of the aesthetic character of an experience, and here I mean any experience not only experiences of art – we are in the first place referring to its quality as a structure, to its coherence. Our feeling for quality is in the first place our feeling for the way the elements composing or comprising an experience fit together. And perhaps the first requirement for anything to be called "beautiful" is that it should exhibit formal coherence of a high order – which assumes, rightly I think, that some structural devices are actually more sophisticated, and so, potentially more richly rewarding because more absorbing and more demanding of our interpretive powers than others. This applies whether we are deciding upon a pair of gardening boots, a wine to go with a meal, the order of words in a sentence or trying to recover what we correctly call our "form" in tennis or some other sport. Concern for coherence is thus not merely a concern for such formal attributes as elegance and balance, but also on occasions a concern with efficiency, for in human designs as in "natural" designs (i.e. animals, plants and insects) there is often a direct relationship between formal coherence and survival. There are those who insist that aesthetic appraisal is concerned with the thing considered in itself rather than in terms of say, its intended use, but if "in itself" it was designed to do something useful our evaluation of its ultimate coherence will be bound to take account of its quality in performance. An elegant spoon that in practice is too shallow to hold soup without spilling it down your shirt fails the coherence test.

Works of Art on the other hand display a very particular and highly characteristic attribute where the criterion of coherence is concerned. For as we have already noted works of art function as signs. And our aesthetic appraisal of works of art will assess coherence not just as order or integrity but as communication. Coherence in works of art is the unity of feeling and form. We expect our experience of the meaning of a work of art to reside, ultimately, in its sensuous form. As we have said already, a work of art affects us as *embodying* meaning, not as pointing towards a meaning that is somehow separable from it. Its meaning is quite literally incarnate. To "read" a work of art then means picking up the clues as to the structural principle informing it and imaginatively reconstructing it as a feeling idea, that is to say, as an evocative image or sign. The appeal of art as sign is to the imagination as Polanyi and Prosch (1976) explain, but image and sign makers must abide by the rules of coherent structure if they are to communicate meaning to us.

All abstractions from experience, all thoughts and concepts, may be accounted for in terms of the imaginative response of the mind: there is a sense in which scientific theories and mathematical models are as much fictions (i.e. products of the imagination) as the works of novelists, dramatists, painters and all other so-called "imitators". (Image has the same latin root as imitation.) However, the imaginative structures, the fictions, made by artists are of a different order from those made, for instance, by scientists. Artists are concerned to generate or stimulate the imagination of the receiver for, to appreciate a work of art, we have to *dwell imaginatively within it*. And to appreciate an imaginative formulation in science this is not so at all. Art works by involving us, evokes a response in our own feeling life. Art's appeal is imaginative. Works of art function as signs that evoke both the recollective and the integrating faculties of imagination. Wordsworth wrote of poetry as "emotion recollected in tranquillity": he was testifying to the evocative or recollective aspect of the impact of a poem. It works by arousing in us a set of images evocative of feelings: it proposes, in its sensate structure, the means of their integration. Poems and other works of art allow the resolution of feeling problems but to do so they must actually evoke feelings. Our response to art is always a feeling response, but feeling qualified imaginatively.

There is a good deal in the literature of creativity to suggest that the key characteristic of the creative mind is not its capacity to *solve* problems (which is, of course, *one* feature) but the capacity to *find* problems. And that doesn't just mean sensing a difficulty or being aware that there is something wrong, that things don't quite fit or make sense. Finding a problem means formulating a problem: expressing it in a form, that is to say giving it a structure which will allow the intelligent relating of the elements that are causing the difficulty. Once arranged into a problematic formulation by means of an idea given intuitively, the relationship of the disparate (i.e. incoherent) elements may be fully worked out and in the solution will be realized as a new perception. A problem form is an hypothesis as to the possibility of integration or coherence. This hypothesis must then be tested and modified until the elements seeking relationship achieve the most perspicuous organization.

It is commonly thought that one of the functions of a work of art is to allow the exploration and integration of complex subjective experiences – the affective consequences of our continuous engagement with the world, and of our being bombarded if you like, by external stimulus. Again, to borrow from Wordsworth, "The World is too much with us". We find respite from the world in those moments of day-dream among which I would number our experience of art. In the day-dreams of art we find the time and space to put ourselves back together, whereas the rush of events in the ordinary, waking world hurry us on so quickly that we cannot make sense of the experiences we undergo and we are left with problems, with incoherences we need to work upon. We need the opportunity to recall sensate disturbance and find coherence in it. Unless we are continually able to remake ourselves in the sense of achieving order, understanding and equilibrium within our world of feeling, we experience ourselves as lost, at odds, out of sorts, on edge, and this condition has inevitable consequences for our behaviour in the world. Our mood affects our motivation: the quality of the energy with which we act in the world.

What I am referring to is not the condition of the emotionally sick, or severely mentally handicapped or disturbed. Not those of us whose affective world has become so confused, so fragmented that we can sustain no kind of meaningful or responsible relationship with the world. Such emotional casualties need special help: therapy at the hands of professionals experienced in assisting the natural processes of healing and re-integration. I am speaking of ordinary people in the normal course of their everyday lives. Of course some of us are more subject to emotional disturbance than others, by virtue of our temperaments, our constitution and particular circumstances. And others live apparently untroubled lives in which there are few excitements and conflicts to ruffle the even flow of subjective experience. But it is contrary to the notion of creative living, to the idea that we are subject to a drive that forbids us, while remaining intelligent and mentally active, to rest on our experiential laurels, our mental achievements – to be satisfied by, to settle for, what we know. We solve one problem, exhaust one interest, only to seek another. Stimulation is the very main-spring of our being – as experiments in sensory deprivation have shown. Mind must have external problems to solve or it turns destructively upon itself.

And every problematic encounter with the object world has its unavoidable consequence for the subject world of feeling. As I have already argued (Ross, 1978) the means available to the ordering of feeling problems, to the production of new feeling structures, new affective possibilities, is our expressive behaviour. And expressive behaviour we define as the reflexive projection of a feeling impulse into a medium. The logic of the way expression works is simple. The mind works by the principle of abstraction: it seeks to represent in some "abstract" form the elements of the structural problems it engages. Objective problems are abstracted into mental representations or concepts which mind then works with in formulating hypotheses about their possible solutions. These mental abstractions may in turn be objectified, represented objectively, in symbolic forms, as in maths, science, engineering etc which facilitate the process of mental problem-solving. Our feeling responses are abstracted mentally as percepts and represented objectively in material forms or "images": expressive behaviour is simply the embodiment of impulse through displacement in the material world of objects. In voice, gesture, facial expression and so forth. When we seek to work upon a feeling problem we must resort to making models in the world of objects that will allow manipulation and playing with formal possibilities, with intuitions of affective coherence.

Abstraction is synonymous with mind. Art works are a particular manifestation of the act of expressive abstraction. They are devised as formulations that might or should permit the integration of feeling and the resolution of sensate disturbance. Essentially this means that they make possible coherent feeling. What disturbance amounts to is the breakdown of affectivity, the blocking of affective ideation. Feeling, in its healthy and active state flows. It flows between being and action. Unresolved feeling problems – sensate disturbances – inhibit the vital flow of feeling that connects us with the world we live in and in which we must operate effectively if we are to survive. We need to work on these feeling problems that inhibit the flow of feeling and so prevent us feeling at home in and at one with the world just as we must work on the conceptual problems that render the world incomprehensible to us as an object and block the reciprocal relationship we seek with it. To resolve sensate difficulties we must be able to abstract from them into natural or man-made sensuous forms. Sensuous forms afford us the feeling ideas we need if we are to maintain subjective stability. Which is why aesthetics stresses not so much function as form – what Margolis means when he says that works of art are artifacts "considered in terms of their design". He is stressing that works of art signify by embodying meaning – by virtue of their sensate qualities. I have proposed that it is sensibility that is the mode of mind that permits the reading and rendering of form as feeling. *Sensibility is intelligent feeling.*

CHAPTER 4

Art and Aesthetics

Aesthetics is the general field of sensuous perception in which sensibility operates; the arts are a sub-division or special instance of aesthetic perception in which such notions as expression and symbolic representation give aesthetic experience a special significance. Arts education has traditionally been dominated by the concept of High Art – a "marginal" commodity prized by an elite minority in society. We need to replace this model of arts education with one embodying principles more in tune with those of a general and comprehensive education.

★   ★   ★   ★   ★

I have argued for a conception of artistic activity as "other" – as belonging to the world of Winnicott's "potential space" in which two subjectivities meet and are personally reconciled through creative, expressive, imaginative action in the object world. I have further suggested that we would be well advised to think of the arts in education, in Leach's terms, as the direct inversion of the ordinary secular curriculum. I now want to turn to consider some of the consequences of this thesis and begin to clarify the way in which I shall use the complementary terms "art" and "aesthetics". Here, I suppose, controversy and contentiousness are finally unavoidable because there can be no such thing as a neutral evaluation or definition of either of these terms. They are both the products of history in the sense that their meanings have changed over time and changed in response to major shifts in the character of our culture. For example, Raymond Williams (1976) has this to say in his account of the "key" word, art:

> "This complex set of historical distinctions between various kinds of human skill and between varying basic purposes in the use of such skills is evidently related to changes in the practical division of labour and to fundamental changes in practical definitions of the purposes of the exercise of skill. It can be primarily related to the changes inherent in capitalist commodity production, with its specialization and reduction of use values to exchange values. There was a consequent defensive specialization of certain skills and purposes to the arts or the humanities where forms of general use and intention which were not determined by immediate exchange could be at least conceptually abstracted." (Page 34)

Williams goes on to point out that for practical purposes we now distinguish the artist on the one hand from the artisan or skilled craftsman – whose "operations" are directly implicated in the world of "exchange values", but, perhaps most obviously, from the scientist and the technologist who are associated with a particular set of skills and purposes related to the mastery or utilization of the object world. By contrast the arts are defined by their apparent commitment to *the expression of subjective states in imaginative creations*. We have inherited these characterizations and it would clearly be a pointless exercise to try to swim against the tide of usage and seek to revive a former emphasis or blur these commonly held distinctions. For example I am never entirely persuaded by science colleagues that the sciences, being both creative and in some senses aesthetic enterprises, offer much the same educational outcomes as the arts – and so, presumably, might do duty for them in a severely curtailed curriculum. Nor do the craft-design-technologists have a case, I feel, as possible substitutes for the visual artists in the curriculum. For all that I am anxious to see both a greater homogeneity in over-all curriculum design and the productive linking of separate disciplines in joint undertakings, that is not to say that I don't regard the arts as a distinctive way of knowing, a special kind of mental discipline that has its own practices to protect and its own outcomes to deliver. So I start where Williams lets his analysis rest: with the arts characterized as essentially "offering to express a generally human (i.e. non-utilitarian) interest", despite the fact, as Willams goes on to point out, that in practice, most artists are treated as a special category of skilled workers "producing a certain kind of marginal commodity". Whilst accepting as basic to art the ideas of human expressivity and the creative imagination, I want to enter a strong disclaimer against any close association between arts education and the world of commodity art. This will need some explanation.

When most people think of arts education they will probably have in mind the Western European traditions of literature, art, classical music and drama. English Literature examination papers test children's responses to books read, under circumstances of free-choice, by a minute fraction of the population. Music exams similarly require knowledge and understanding of a musical repertoire as foreign to the interests of ordinary people as the further reaches of relativity theory and computer science. Children are earnestly paraded through the Royal Academy's Stanley Spencer Exhibition at all ages from 6 to 16, presumably on the assumption that this is time and money properly spent in the interest of their art education. They are likewise bussed to the theatre and the concert hall to sit somewhat awkwardly amidst the arts aficionados. I am not here concerned to knock either the art-commodity market or the patronage and practice of the High or Fine arts. However, I do want to challenge the prevalent assumption that arts education – no matter what allowance is made for personal creativity at the child's own level –

should be an induction into the artistic predilections of a privileged social minority. This is scarcely an adequate let alone an appropriate basis for the kind of general arts education that has been widely advocated, and by many teachers endorsed, over the past twenty or thirty years.

My own feeling is that despite the emphasis now being placed upon creative *participation* in the arts by perhaps the majority of arts teachers in schools, the assumption that the standards are set in and allegiance owed ultimately to the High Art World goes very deep (and the High Art World is now entirely identified with art as exchange-value, as commodity). I doubt very much whether we can ever achieve the kind of arts education practice we need whilst this assumption prevails. But if music education is not ultimately about Beethoven and Bach (or Cage and Stockhausen), if art education is not about Rembrandt and Picasso, if drama doesn't mean Shakespeare, and English Literature, Lawrence and Hopkins, what on earth are to be our models, our standards, our criteria of relevance and excellence? If the familiar world celebrated in and exemplified by the main courses we ourselves followed at college and university is to be rejected as irrelevant to the school situation, to education in general, what *is* our business to be? Where are we to find the content for the arts curriculum? I think we have to begin by getting out from beneath the shadow of the Realized Form – the Great Work of Art. Now that must sound very odd coming after a perhaps unnecessarily elaborate argument in support of an essentially art-based, "aesthetic" curriculum. Nevertheless I am sure this is the way to proceed and I don't sense any ultimate contradiction.

I shall, in fact, want to bring back the Realized Forms of High (Class) Art eventually, however, in a fundamentally realigned and restructured arts curriculum where they will have a significant but not a determining role. As it is we are petrified by the gorgon Art has become – which is why one can easily understand, for example, the instrumentalist retreat from the aesthetic in seeking a more effective and a more legitimate role for the arts in education. But I still maintain they are wrong. In rejecting the dominion of the Great Works of Art – and, by implication, of the Famous Artist – I am not turning my back on the aesthetic principle, far from it. I hope to be able to show why the aesthetic principle is the correct basis for an arts curriculum and how the exaltation of the aesthetic can actually be achieved without either violating the democratic principle now widely held amongst arts educators or joining the queues at the Tate or at the National Theatre. Without subscribing to the view that we are somehow in the business of marketing High Art if only in as much as we are softening up potential future consumers. We already recognize that we must not allow potential future practitioners to slip through our fingers and of course, there is nothing inherently wrong with either notion provided that they remain attendant upon rather than central to our prime concerns as arts educators.

Anyone now working in the art commodity market is suspect since that market is exclusive to a small section of the community. Today's artist-in-residence suffocates under the mantle of the Great Tradition and probably attracts only the curiosity of those amongst whom he or she resides. We cannot afford to allow our work to be dominated by the Artist and his or her Work of Art because they both bespeak a role for aesthetic experience that is peripheral not in the positive sense which I have already discussed, but because it is beyond the ken of the people. Great Works of Art have become minority (Williams called them "marginal") commodities. Reverence for Art condemns children to feeling inadequate, to taking as "good" what others apparently value but in which they themselves can see or for which they can feel nothing intrinsically satisfying. In other words it invites them to forfeit precisely that faculty of intuitive judgement which we ought to be protecting and nurturing in everything they do. Further, children, especially of course children growing up in a multi-cultural society such as ours increasingly is, are only too well aware that the Artist has nothing directly to do with them, or their families, the places they live in, even the times they live in. And if that is what arts education really means then of course it is prodigiously irrelevant. Attendant upon the worship of the Artist is a particular attitude towards the arts, towards poetry and music, towards the "poetic" as being somehow foreign to the experience of ordinary people at least some of the time. All right for teachers and vicars and such like and of course only to be expected at school where their values are the dominant ones anyway, but a waste of time for anyone else. Again I think I can reasonably claim that this sort of attribution of "abnormality" has nothing to do with the actual character of aesthetic activity which is, rather, socially, even economically, derived. I have already said that I want to insist upon the "otherness" of art, but that does not mean that art somehow belongs to other people – i.e. to the Artist and the Arts Council and people who read Shakespeare, drink in the Saloon Bar and get invited to Royal Garden Parties.

This probably comes across as a very crude and boringly familiar assault upon middle-class, bourgeois values and I shall stand accused of hypocrisy since those values are inevitably my own. My concern however is to identify and eliminate what I take to be one of the major constraints upon arts education at the present time. I believe that this deep-rooted subservience to the World of High Art is what not only invalidates a great deal of art, drama, music and English teaching but also vitiates much recent writing about the arts in education where such concepts as "connoisseurship" and "excellence" are being canvassed as allegedly powerful devices in rescuing the arts from the ravages wrought by unbridled subjectivism and the garbage left behind by the receding tide of creative self-expression in the schools. The arts cannot possibly be defended as "other" in the sense of belonging to the better-off. Every foray amongst the hoi-poloi by High Art missionaries, every High Art

placement is doomed, like a sudden fall of snow in June. It is also I feel both
politically and morally suspect.

The basis of arts education, in John Dewey's words, is Experience. And it
is towards an account of art as experience that I now proceed. I am going to
propose that it is as *aesthetic knowing* that art achieves its legitimacy in the
curriculum. And aesthetic knowing is nothing other than the exercise of
sensibility. "Sensibility" and "aesthetics" are, like "art", also numbered
among Raymond Williams's key words and I shall turn to this analysis for help
with both words. Again it will be useful to quote him at length.

> "It is clear from this history that *aesthetic* with its specialized references to art, to
> visual appearance and to a category of what is "fine" or "beautiful" is a key
> formation in a group of meanings which at once emphasized and isolated
> subjective sense-activity as the basis of art and beauty as distinct, for example,
> from social or cultural interpretations. It is an element in the divided modern
> consciousness of art and society: a reference beyond social use and social
> valuation which, like one special meaning of culture, is intended to express a
> human dimension which the dominant version of society appears to exclude. The
> emphasis is understandable but the isolation can be damaging, for there is
> something irresistibly displaced and marginal about the now common and
> limiting phrase "aesthetic considerations", especially when contrasted with
> practical or utilitarian considerations, which are elements of the same basic
> division." (Page 28)

Once again we find the emphasis, as with the word "art", upon the expression
of the "human dimension" and the marginality that ensues upon the
separation of the aesthetic from the practical aspects of experience. I want to
repeat what has already been said about the need to distinguish between the
quite proper and indeed fruitful description of the arts as other (at the edge),
and the displacement of aesthetic and religious experience to the margin of
contemporary consciousness. I cannot accept that it is either reasonable or
desirable that being the odd man should necessarily entail being the odd man
"out". Earlier in the Williams discussion the aesthetic is seen as fundamentally associated with sensation – and hence – by implication, with perception.
The literature abounds with accounts and definitions of the aesthetic and, as I
have already indicated, provides sufficient cause for seemingly endless
contention. We cannot avoid crossing this perilous ground but, that said, I
don't think we need loiter over-long. We need simply to emphasize the
enactive aspect of perception in reinforcement of our claim that aesthetic
knowing is the discerning or perception of sensate order – the making sense
of, the discerning of coherence in sensuous and mental phenomena. If this is
the function of sensibility then the reward or pleasure to be derived from the
perception of coherence will be qualitatively related to the level of ordering
achieved. Which means that we shall be aware that some coherences achieve
more satisfying levels of organization than others and that we shall want to
ascribe especial aesthetic value to them. As Williams says such categories as

"fine" and "beautiful" are traditional terms of commendation in aesthetics and it would seem reasonable to equate the beautiful with the particularly intense pleasure that we have in our perception of higher level coherences. Which is one way of saying that the aesthetic consideration is the consideration of formal quality – essentially of the level of formal integration – as distinct, for instance, from the practical serviceability of the phenomenon under consideration.

Although any object or artifact, from a cricket bat to a nuclear missile, from a musical score to a scientific formula, as subject to perception may also be the subject of aesthetic appraisal in terms of the quality or level of its structural coherence (which would naturally include a consideration of the object as an example of its kind, i.e. in relation to the tradition or field from which it was derived), the arts have a special relationship with the aesthetic in as much as they both share what Williams calls *the intention to express the "human dimension"*. Aesthetic education has to be rooted in the operation of sensibility, in the feeling for form, for all forms, natural and functional, material and mental. I am indebted to Keith Swanwick for suggesting that the twin features of sensibility are "perspicuity" and "poignancy". Both refer to "sharp" discernment, the one of form and the other of feeling. Art education fosters the deployment of sensibility not merely in the design and discernment of good (coherent) form but in the evoking of human sign, in the making of significant forms. When we flick our consciousness over from viewing to envisioning we move from form to sign. Art by my definition becomes a special deployment of the aesthetic response – demanding a special focus of sensibility, a particular way of seeing. However whereas we may properly say, "If it's art it must be aesthetic", we may not say "If it's aesthetic it must be art". On this account we might want to say that although arts education were necessarily aesthetic, aesthetic education would not be restricted to the consideration of or be merely identified with the arts. It would also follow that it would be possible, even if undesirable, to create a programme of aesthetic education that need give no special weight to the arts. Since I have defined the arts as a special use of the aesthetic response and based my account of artistic experience upon the concept of aesthetic perception it would seem reasonable to group the arts together under the broader heading of aesthetic education and to set about supporting a cross-curricular commitment to the enhancement of sensibility. If the object of aesthetic education is the enhancement of sensibility, i.e. the individual's capacity to perceive coherence in sensuous and mental form, art education is distinguished as sensibility mobilized in the service of the expressive impulse. Artistic perception finds poetic meaning embodied in sensuous forms.

If we are to push out the Famous Artist and the High Art Tradition – what kind of art do we have in mind? What might our touchstone be? And the answer has to be: *the arts of the people*. The popular or vernacular arts. I shall immediately be asked if I am talking about teenage pop-music and subculture and would have to reply no, or not merely that. In the sense that I am not advocating either the substitution of teenage music for the traditional repertoire of the Famous Composers or the subjection of teenage music to the technical analysis of the musicologist. Perhaps I can best explain what I have in mind by taking as an example, a musical occasion, from a very different culture than ours. In the small village communities in Brunei it is still customary to make communal music to celebrate a wedding. The musical material is traditional and handed down orally from generation to generation. The men dance and sing – perhaps a love-song appropriate to the occasion – and the women of the village encircle them, accompanying the singing and dancing with drumming. I am told that there has to be some "rapport" between the dancers and the singers, otherwise the artistic event lacks life, and it is not unusual for the girls to demand a different set of dancers – ones they might feel more in tune with! The tunes are customarily simple and the songs have a sustained, happy, untroubled quality about them – you feel they could just go on and on. In some cases they do. I am told by a Bruneian friend that the music is reflective of the village society and its way of life: it is a more or less classless community, so the music itself has a strikingly homogeneous quality. Life is happy, placid and regular: work in the paddy fields for everyone by day, and recreation and rest by night. People are at pains to get on with each other and no one suffers hardship, misfortune or sickness alone. The community gives its music an unmistakable quality of conviviality.

What are the characteristics of a genuinely popular art form such as I have just described? It seems to have several salient features. It is expressive of communal coherence, mutuality and solidarity – it is in itself a socially cohesive force. It gives at least even weight to performance and to spectating with perhaps the main emphasis upon a generally high level of participation. It seems to be committed to the interactive principle, among the performers, e.g. the singers and dancers, and between performers and audience. (There are many examples of the disturbing effects upon western actors of having to perform before highly interactive audiences in Africa and South America.) Leaders and "artists" seem little in evidence, popular artists tending to work anonymously or collectively, not so much startling or shocking society with the novelty of their work as delighting by their skill, both in the techniques of their performance and in interpreting largely familiar material. Which anticipates the next point: the sense that art is a timeless dimension of everyday experience, giving continuity and a sense of connection across the generations. Popular art is embedded in what Williams calls the "values of use" rather than the "values of exchange" – works of popular art are not, customarily, commodities for barter or for prestigious possession. It is only royalty that attaches "exchange" value to artifacts in societies such as the one I have just referred to. Popular art is popularly esteemed, felt to be intrinsically worthwhile – might well be embedded in other practices of a "sacred" nature that lend it even greater moment. Whether this is so or not it is not noticeably contextualized: it is homogeneous with the life of the people. Further it is characterized by the qualities of continuity and spontaneity: that is to say it has a cyclical rather than a periodic feel and tends to avoid climax and other dramatic effects, and the life of any particular performance is likely to be the interpretive spark of the performance rather than any rigid obedience to rule or convention. There will however be a serious respect for the traditional form.

These then are some of the characteristics of the kind of popular art, art of the people, that I am interested in. I don't claim the list to be exhaustive. We might present them in table form, with their opposites ranged alongside them. What I am suggesting is that the opposite values and concepts are those by which the High Art of the West is dominated and controlled:

Vernacular	*High Arts*
Organic	Artificial
Self-evaluating	Other-evaluated
Participation	Mystifying
Use value	Exchange value
Cyclical	Spasmodic
Continuous	Fragmented
Cohesive	Divisive
Convivial	Competitive
Inter-active	Private
Local	General
Gratuitous	Implicated
Staple	Luxury
Democratic	Autocratic
Collective	Patronized
Spontaneous	Commissioned
Intimate	Distanced
Profane	Polite
Changing	Fixed
Adapting	Conserving

If it is true that the truly popular arts are distinguished in the ways I have been suggesting then it will be clear why I believe that the vernacular principle has more to offer a general arts education than the traditional subservience to the High Arts, and even if it is easier to find examples of popular art flourishing in the non-industrialized, so-called, under-developed countries of the world, than within our own contemporary society – and I am not persuaded that this really is the case – that is no reason for suggesting that my thesis is fundamentally either mistaken or outmoded. I want to make it quite clear that I am not merely harking back to some illusory golden age in the past. I am saying, let us abstract the qualities of the traditional popular arts, surviving or defunct, and use them as the criteria by which to establish and evaluate a genuinely comprehensive arts education. If there are popular arts practices extant within our society then it is to these we should turn for inspiration and for confirmation. What I now want to do is to look again at the criteria I have identified and see what they might mean when transferred to the province of arts education.

A glance down the two columns will suffice to underline my point about the arts curriculum being the "direct inversion" of the normal curriculum. The concepts and values presented in the "popular" column form a profile that could hardly be more at variance with the central, time-bound, secular character of the curriculum as a whole. What may be a little surprising is to realize the extent to which a High Art curriculum can be accommodated within and identified with traditional educational aims and methods. Perhaps we should not be so surprised because, of course, the more strikingly participatory features of arts education and the heuristic discovery and play methods found in junior schools and to a limited extent in secondary schools, have been introduced only relatively recently and are by no means the norm. The familiar Eng. Lit. syllabus, and even some of the new drama syllabuses are still emphatically "academic" in character and reward academic (i.e. verbal-analytical) skills. Music education is largely dominated by the academic principle. Only art seems to have made the switch from spectating to creating, but I sense even there, as children move up through the school system, we have increasing subservience to a studio/art college ethic with each child-as-artist seen as an albeit naïve and untutored Artist producing artifacts in a competitive, other-valued and commodity-based milieu; that is when they are not actually being encouraged to see themselves as specialized or skilled operatives with a market awaiting them. The Design School of art education has replaced the frivolous and romantic idea of the Artist with the more acceptable face of the Engineer. What I am saying is that from this analysis it is already clear how extensive have been the concessions made by the arts in finding a legitimate place within the normal, secular curriculum. The current "outsider" status of traditional arts education tallies with the middle-class view of art as High Art: as marginal. It draws no strength at all from the left-handed, "sinister" and even "occult" character of the popular arts that are at once an essential thread in the life of the people and at the same time the source of an illicit, dionysian energy – in which fiction is somehow truer than fact. Art as a genuinely revolutionary life force. D.H. Lawrence (1952) asks,

"Why has mankind had such a craving to be imposed upon? Why this lust after imposing creeds, imposing deeds, imposing buildings, imposing language, imposing works of art? The thing becomes an imposition and a weariness at last. Give us things that are alive and flexible, which won't last too long and become an obstruction and a weariness. Even Michelangelo becomes at last a lump and a burden and a bore. It is so hard to see past him."

We need a general arts education that respects the otherness, the sacred character of art and at the same time lays claim to the immediacy, the "usefulness" of the vernacular tradition. We have to repudiate the deep-seated notion that the purpose of arts education is to initiate the young into the World of High Art, with its profane commitment to status values and the commodity principle. We need to concentrate upon improving attitudes and perceptions rather than artifacts and products.

CHAPTER 5

The Vernacular Principle

The vernacular or popular arts are explored as embodying principles
appropriate to a general aesthetic education.

★   ★   ★   ★   ★

If we were fully to implement the vernacular idea in arts education, what
would it mean in practical terms? Well, I suspect it would make for
considerable changes in many different areas and, not least, give the most
awful box on the ears to the whole lamentable business of arts teacher
training. At the moment student teachers follow main courses in the arts that
are dominated by the High Art ethic. They practise the high performance
skills of the concert soloist or orchestral player; they study the received text
of the Eng. Lit. drama syllabus and are trained in the practical skills of
theatrical performance; they become print-makers, studio potters (not "real"
potters be it noted), painters in the idiom of last year's shows at the Heywood
Gallery or the Royal Academy. I suggest that not only does such training
contribute at best negligibly to the skills the student would need to teach by
the populist principle, but that such experiences are themselves actually
crippling in as much as they endorse the values of the High Art system. A
vernacular arts education would encourage work that was individual but not
private. Work that was animated and inspired by the twin principles of
participation and spontaneity. It would be committed to motivating all
children to join in, enjoy themselves and do well – in the sense of giving and
gaining what they personally valued. It would be designed to be intrinsically
satisfying and significant, there and then. It would entail the acquisition of
such technical and creative skills as were necessary to full participation. It
would be fundamentally non-competitive: children would neither be graded
nor banded. Neither would sharp nor rigid divisions be drawn between one
arts area and another. It would need teachers who were able and ready both
to create the potential space, the boundary zone, for their students and to join
them in playing within it. Products and performances would be shared and
"given" away, or exchanged as one exchanges gifts. There would be no
"norm referenced" general public examination in the arts, and all forms of
external examination or monitoring would be highly suspect. There could be

no "nationally agreed" general arts curriculum beyond the laying down of broad principles and criteria. Children would be their own evaluators and participate in the keeping of records. The work itself would require conditions supportive of continuity, and of cyclical patterns of creation and response, so as to encourage sustained work, give due recognition to the importance of unconscious forces and processes, discourage purely reactive, ejaculatory and fragmented experience: reward engagement rather than productivity.

It would, perhaps above all else be committed to the gratuitous principle – to the idea of freedom. To what I have already called "life abundant". And the value and necessity of hard work would be self-evident and would be sensed as the creative, expressive, world-changing and life-enhancing principle that it essentially is. Not work in the enslaving, divesting, exchange-dominated form with which the developed countries are now all too familiar. It would be dominated by material (sensual!) media and would witness the constant fashioning and significating of materials – rather than by the word. Criticism and analysis would serve the ends of perception, and perception, vision itself, would be the prized outcome to which everything in the arts curriculum was geared. Accessibility would be preferred to reverence and where access was expensive then money would have to be found that would admit the many, rather than separate out the few. It would embody the concerns of and be responsible to local people – the people of a particular place: its artifacts would not necessarily be of other than curiosity value to anyone else.

What I am advocating to all levels of education is a general, that is to say, a non-esoteric arts education for all, based on the thesis that we are, indeed, all artists and that the arts, as a universal phenomenon of human experience, play a unique role in the healthy, the holy life of a people. When I say that everyone is an artist, I mean everyone is a maker (a poet) of some sort, addicted to quality, liable to let objects and spectacle possess them (rather than the other way round). I mean that we are inveterately iconic: sign-makers and sign-readers. And that the artistic perspective adapts sensibility to the "art" of sign-making. Vernacular art, like play and like day-dreaming, serves the vital function, in Winnicott's words, of allowing a healthy accommodation between subject and object words. It is "natural" in the sense that no-one would question or closely enquire into either its value or its legitimacy. It serves understanding by direct and intuitive means and it makes sense imaginatively, that is to say by allowing experience to be dissolved and reconstituted upon affective rather than rational principles.

It is a way of knowing which must be continually reinforced, despite its naturalness and its deep-rootedness for, as we shall see, it is a cultural form constituted according to convention, and has to compete with other such forms of human expression and communication. Cultural specificity becomes immediately apparent when we try to appreciate, for example, the dancing of an alien culture: we sense that, despite the perhaps attractive and stimulating effect of the movements we are watching, they are foreign to us, designed by and for a different sensibility. I prefer to see art as an outlook or orientation of being, rather than as a class of objects in the world. This becomes critical for work in school. Most secondary school arts teachers know at first hand the problems that arise when their pupils have the "wrong" attitude to arts work, when they become fixated upon the purely pragmatic and regard, for example, the imaginative mode as wasteful, irrelevant, perhaps even disconcerting since most of them gave it up with childhood itself. They need initiating too into the skills and traditions that have become associated with the different art forms, not, of course, in order that they may be subjected to self-justifying tests of memory or practice but so that they may actually be able to engage in and use the arts in question. By initiation of course I mean teaching.

If one of the major tasks facing us is to realign arts education upon a more appropriate theoretical base – what I have called "adopting the vernacular principle" – then there is another, equally important issue that needs to be faced up to and resolved: that is to say what we might actually mean by "teaching" in the arts. For there are those who would argue that you cannot teach art; that somehow the artistic response is, if not exactly a simple question of talent, then at least, like divine grace, somewhat unpredictable and erratic in its distribution. We are not all, they say, nor can we all expect to be equally favoured. So you just give the children brushes and paints to dabble about with in the hope that they won't really come to harm and might actually find that they can do something pleasant.

One version of this approach is caricatured under the description of "Free-Expression". Free-expression has been getting a universally bad press and this is both important and unfortunate. It is important because the concept does in fact have a very great deal to offer arts education – especially when construed as the removing of inhibitors (both personal and cultural) to the expression of thought, feeling, and personality. You are contemptuous of free-expression only if you are unaware of the damage done in our society and in our schools, by the embargo, actual or implicit, upon the expressive mode. It is unfair because into the free-expression sin bin are cast all those disciplined and daring acts that defy classification and evaluation as recognizable art products. The vital emphasis upon process in arts education has been quite unfairly scape-goated as encouraging what is decried in some quarters as a kind of aimless and mindless self-indulgence. As I say, this is unfair because it takes process and its admittedly messy detritus out of context, and purports to evaluate it on what have to be fundamentally inappropriate criteria. Whilst I would want to agree with those who are up in arms against aimlessness and self-indulgence in arts education, I wouldn't equate them either with the general term Expression, or the now disparaging term, Free-Expression. It is not hard of course to guess why any reference to expression would give the shakes to the centralists, the pragmatists.

As I say, the notion of teaching the arts needs re-examining and re-defining: in particular the whole question of the teacher's role in respect of the student's creativity and maturing sensibility. How to foster perspicuity and poignancy. We shall be considering some practical examples later in this essay: what perhaps we need to do here is to see what the practical implications of the "populist" approach would mean in a school and for individual arts teachers.

The first thing that needs saying is that at every level of education from nursery to sixth form college and beyond there should be a policy for the arts – or better still for "aesthetic education". A good deal of what I have been saying in this chapter might find a place in such a policy statement. The basic idea would be that what gives identity and cohesion to the aesthetic area in education is *the principle of design:* that is to say man's sensuous perception of form, of shapes and structures, and the demand for qualitative coherence. The aesthetic is also a communication system (a code) and artistic significa-tion derives from the embodiment or location of feeling in sensuous forms. The policy for aesthetic education would specify a general cross-curricular interest in all forms of design and in the appreciation of qualitative coherence everywhere; it would also entail a particular concern for aesthetic expression and "communication" in the arts.

Every school must have someone with the right knowledge and under-standing capable of taking responsibility for the pupils' aesthetic education and capable of co-ordinating the work of other teachers. The extent to which the policy needs to be elaborated in terms of the actions of other members of staff will depend upon the educational level of any particular institution. In the nursery school for instance one would hope that the teacher in charge would have at least a basic understanding of what was meant by aesthetic perception and appraisal, would see some way of articulating this dimension of education for other staff and would perhaps be on the look out to encourage another teacher to take a special interest in this area, making sure for instance that the environment itself was intelligently designed for learning and living, that there was plenty of good sensory stimulus available, that creative play using a wide range of different expressive media was very much at a premium. Children are both intensely sensuous and freely creative in the nursery and early primary years, and resourcing and encouraging their aesthetic development is of absolutely crucial importance. Primary and secondary schools both need teachers to co-ordinate policy-making and teaching in the aesthetic area – as well as specialists, or specially-trained personnel, available to give proper instruction in the handling of particular media and art forms. Teachers who describe themselves as merely "dabblers" will never be able to grasp the problems facing children or be in a position to teach children ways of moving their work on. And this is one of the major shortcomings of arts education at both primary and secondary levels. Many teachers are self-confessed ignoramuses as far as the arts are concerned, so one wonders what, beyond the making of Mothers Day Cards and paper chains, ought reasonably to be expected of them.

At secondary level, the studio and academy (not to say the academic) backgrounds of many so-called specialists, in no way equip them to understand or assist in the child's creative work. They are simply lost because unqualified, and incompetent. The skills required, for example, to help individuals or groups create authentic forms in drama or music or art are simply not there. It is almost as if no-one has ever stopped to ask what form such skills might take. The ducks-to-water act of blind faith upon which so much arts education is based is in fact an abrogation of pedagogic responsibility. But I am running ahead of myself. Having a policy for aesthetic education means making a coherent statement about the nature and scope of aesthetic experience, about the school's provision for aesthetic development (another topic barely understood within the profession) and including an account of the criteria by which student progress will be assessed. We shall be taking a closer look at the form such a statement might take – and will have to say rather more on the issues both of aesthetic development and assessment criteria. My intention for the moment is simply to make a number of general points in connection with what I have called the implications of implementing the vernacular principle in aesthetic education. Schools need policies – essentially one policy for the entire aesthetic area. In as much as the principle of "good design" spans the whole curriculum, the aesthetic policy statement should be comprehensible to all other teachers (not to say parents and children) – and schools will need to consider how this concern for quality of design can be assimilated into those areas of the curriculum not directly implicated in arts teaching.

Beyond this cross-curricular concern with "artifacts apprehended in terms of their design" is the involvement with the arts themselves. The vernacular principle lays special obligations upon us – the most trenchant of which might be that arts education should be seen as participatory, as inter-active and as cohesive. Within the aesthetics team – if a school can run to such – the arts people would have perhaps the central responsibility. For all that many non-arts teachers have interests that overlap with the aesthetic emphasis upon design, none of them is involved in that special area within the aesthetic namely sensuous communication through sign-making, the aesthetic's expressive or poetic dimension. The arts team within the aesthetic faculty needs to be large enough to make an impact, but it must also itself be coherently constituted otherwise it cannot possibly be effective. Given such a team then the basic philosophy outlined above has to be generally accepted. You can't for instance, have the musicians sticking out for the Lives of the Great Composers and an Introduction to Webern for the examination stream, and the rest nowhere.

What does our "vernacular" principle mean for the individual arts teacher? Use-value means that the children must sense they are using, able to make use of, the arts as relevant to their own lives; as intrinsically valuable. We are talking here about the qualities of immediacy and directness. The creative process has to be as absorbing, as entrancing and as rewarding as the pretend-play of the three-year-old; the child's appreciative experience of pictures, poems, plays and musical pieces must be similarly absorbing, entrancing and rewarding. Again think of the rapt attention of the nursery child at "story time" – whether at school or on mother's lap. Growing up aesthetically means gradually becoming confident enough to lose oneself in one's creative day dreams – as maker, performer or audience. This is the sense in which I would expect the arts to have use-value. The arts, to adopt Keats' words, are "Magic casements". Marcuse prefers other terms: he writes of the arts as affording us "alternative realities" – fictions somehow truer than the actuality of life experience. Not useful in the narrow sense of making toothbrush racks or oven cloths – not of course that there is anything inherently wrong with either! It's just that such is not the use of art. Art is sign.

You can tell instantly which children are using art in the way I mean: it is plainly evident in their faces and bodies as a quality of engagement and motivation. What Gaston Bachelard (1958) calls "the dream values" (Page 17). When you are really using art you are not analysing it or making judgements about it or "interpreting" it, in the sense of finding some verbal equivalent for it. You are living it. You are day-dreaming, possessed by the form, absorbed, penetrated by, suffused with its aesthetic. Which means, for example, in presenting works of art (both Famous and Popular) to children, we seek to excite and sharpen their sensibility so that they are not playing detectives but dreaming the sound, not identifying the trombone or the diminished seventh, but being spaced by it, being timed by it, being extended, composed, wrapped up, caressed, seared, shocked by it. "Seeing" shapes, figures, scenes – recalled and suggested. Getting up to move, dance – representing their sensations in colour and line – in "poetic" words. Whatever makes the listener richer, more sensuous – whatever unlocks, releases the work's aesthetic, such that the child is carried away. In music we sound the subjective world. Make and take "soundings".

Participation is another key principle for us – closely allied of course with this notion of the use of art. The word I have selected as its opposite is mystification and what I want to get at is the idea that art as an aspect of human experience is not something out there, something privileged that belongs to the rich, or the spiritually gifted, or to the lunatic fringe, or to the academic minority who have made it their special study. Art is something we must all have a stake in, must all be able to use more or less immediately, and need to use rather than, say, either worship, or enshrine or give a wide berth to. So the emphasis of a vernacular arts curriculum will be upon access and competence: children will be able to get involved, to look at, watch and read the things that turn them on – as opposed for example to being equipped to appreciate so-called "good" writing and/or "good" music when they are older. This latter alternative should not be lightly dismissed: it is a very prevalent notion concerning arts education, if not among arts teachers themselves then certainly amongst non-arts Heads, parents and governors. "Graft now – pleasure later" is a recipe for disaster where arts education is concerned. It has to be the day-dream now, this time, every time. So, art is not to be a mystification.

But neither is the arts education process. The spirit of participation must run clean through everything the teacher and the class do together. The children participate in the planning of the curriculum, in the selection of activities, in the evaluation of the process; the teacher's participation is welcomed by the children in their decisions and aesthetic judgements as a way of educating them. This does not mean that the teacher subverts the child's authority when it counts – simply that there is a crucially participatory role for the teacher in learning rather than a principally authoritarian or autocratic role. Such are the constituents of day-dreaming that certain options are closed to the teacher. For instance, you have to be careful not to "wake" the child – the teacher's clumsiness, insensitivity, nervousness and insecurity, all threaten the dreamer, cloud the numinous. And then there is the downright destructiveness of the uncomprehending adult who simply treads all over the child's dreams. If my language evokes altogether too soft, too romantic an image, then I have failed to do justice to my conception – which is that the principle of participation in arts education requires high levels of understanding and practical discipline from teacher and pupil alike. It is in fact much easier – and much sloppier – to conduct arts education on the principle of mutual aloofness and non-involvement which takes one of two forms: the authoritarian or the *laissez-faire*. Either, I tell you what counts, you do it, then I let you know the score. Or, here's the materials – just carry on. And, because it is easier and because so many teachers know no better, these things happen all the time.

By interaction I mean the principle of reciprocation, of reciprocity between teacher and pupil, pupil and pupil, maker and medium, school and community. It is essentially the principle of conviviality, of inter-relatedness of the members of a community, of man and environment. If the use of art is in the first place a matter of personal, of individual response, it remains somehow sterile, unconsummated until it achieves contextualization – until it achieves cultural, that is to say social resonance. Aesthetic education is embodied in mutuality in as much as the drive to compare our evaluations, to *share* our insights and delights with others, constitutes a vital aspect of the expressive principle.

Again, the whole question of evaluation is so important that it must be treated separately; however, it will suffice for the moment simply to point out that there can be no satisfactory personal evaluation that does not find an echo, its corroboration, beyond the self. Most of us are very well aware of the compulsion to draw others into our experiences, say, of the beautiful and the meaningful – our experience of the coherent at whatever level and in whatever domain of experience. "Come and taste this", we say. "Quickly! Come to the window. Look at the sky!" "Daddy, come and see what I've made!" "Listen to this!" "Get that!" We need the corroboration of others. There are people who disclaim such feelings, such inclinations to share their experience with others in the world. But I would agree with Gaston Bachelard "We must give exterior destiny to the interior being". (Page 11) Maybe there is nothing wrong with expressive reticence, and yet for those who do admit to such an impulse, the accompanying sense of freedom and of fruitfulness is reinforcement enough. They sense that a world not shared is somehow sterile. Denied its "exterior destiny", our aesthetic response remains unrealized, unsatisfied. My own view of the matter is that the urge to share, to invite the appreciation of the other, derives essentially from our early experience of that mutual world of the "potential space" – and that we never lose the desire to find again the "good-enough", the perfect stranger, amongst the companions of later separated being, with whom to share and by virtue of whom to confirm, to authorize our subjectivity. The creative process (Ross, 1978) includes the moment of evaluation: the impulse to evaluate is as strong, as urgent, as the impulse to resolve the sensate disturbance. It is not so much that what we seek is another's approval – it is that their approval of the maker goes without saying, is not in question. We tend to seek out in our shared moments those whose personal regard for us is not in question, in order that we may be absolutely open in our own judgement and expression of what we have seen or done. Furthermore by passing on what I feel subjectively, by giving it an "external destiny", I give it being, establish it phenomenologically. I render it perceptible ("I am because I am perceived to be").

It is admittedly a puzzling subject: it is nevertheless interesting as a feature of human aesthetic behaviour for all that. We acknowledge in the principle of inter-action our dependence upon the world, the other, in our making and in our celebrating. We equate conviviality as well we might, with the principles of fertility and creativity. Our being is established in that interactive space where our subjectivity encounters and merges with the subjectivity of the other. I and thou.

By *cohesiveness* I mean not simply the ethos of the collective, I mean the tendency towards collaboration and the blurring of boundaries – among the arts, between the arts and the rest of the curriculum. The popular arts do not stress specialization or separatism: their tendency is towards social cohesion and this is effective through a readiness to participate and to interact. The hall-mark of a cohesive approach to arts education would be the children's sense of their arts teachers as a team of collaborators mediating essentially complementary experiences. There would be numerous occasions when the different arts teachers would be seen and experienced as working together and when specialists in one medium would encourage exploration in other media. As for the pupils, they would have a similar sense of shared purpose one with another.

People are attracted to certain media and certain ways of working (large, small, fine, bold, active, contemplative) and, it has been suggested, are usually dominated by either dramatic or depictive representational strategies. This latter notion is clearly borne out in the observation of young children at play: some are strikingly dramatic, creating characters out of objects and manipulating them in simulated situations, others using objects to create visual rather than dramatic effects, taking eagerly to graphic forms of representation as soon as their powers of manipulation and co-ordination will allow. Given these temperamental preferences we shall neither wish nor expect children to be polymaths in the arts, though there is undoubted scope for raising the all-rounder's level of performance. Children will want to make not only their own marks but to "mark" in their own ways – and work in sound, for example, will be organized on principles peculiar to that medium. Furthermore there can be no simple paraphrasing from one medium to another. Musical experience makes its own impact and makes its own demands. There is an important sense in which we don't expect to find one medium as good as another. We may be provoked by a common stimulus but meaning in music will always be different from meaning in visual or kinetic or verbal forms.

Whilst respecting the integrity of the separate arts a vernacular arts curriculum would stress the community or commonwealth of the arts and so would be constantly reinforcing their common roots in human need and human expression as well as their social and political identity within the school. As a corollary of this attitude the work itself would tend to stress continuity, would exhibit a timeless, organic quality as opposed to a frantic flitting from snippet to snippet, eruption to eruption. The working atmosphere would be calm but not repressive, exciting but not frantic; subject matter would be basic, archetypal in feel, even if evidently local and topical at the levels of surface or stimulus; aesthetic development would be gradual, long-term, and curriculum objectives similarly identified by taking the long view. Interruption of the slowly unfolding process of development either from within or beyond the school could not be countenanced. Cohesiveness would show in the pupils' work-rhythm and in their perception of their own aesthetic development as coherent, integral and authentic.

I have outlined what I see as the distinguishing principles characteristic of a "vernacular" arts curriculum. At this point I shall not enlarge upon those principles beyond making just one or two points of clarification. A vernacular arts curriculum would, as I have said, look especially to those art forms that traditionally and currently engage the people at large as models for the kinds of activities we would be promoting in schools. There is a sense in which "content" would take care of itself in a truly convivial setting – in much the same way as the "content" of a dramatic or musical improvization is discovered in the playing. I believe that provided the teacher has a firm conceptual and technical grasp of what constitutes significant forming in a particular medium – or group of media – starting points, themes, output may (indeed *should*) be particular and unique for every group on every occasion and are quintessentially unpredictable. So there would be no point in writing an elaborated syllabus (and no possibility of agreeing upon a national one). All the arts teacher need do is to confront the class with media and the possibility of sensuous forming: the "problems" to be worked would be discovered "on the job" by individuals within the group and by the group as a whole. So we have an original, organic, spontaneous curriculum: one that is new for every group, every generation of children. Only the basic principles of sensuous forming would provide the continuity and bed-rock of the work. Principles interpreted differently for different groups, with different needs and abilities.

I have proposed that the arts curriculum be considered as having three related facets or dimensions:

1. The Academic: the study of art.
2. The Practical: learning the technical skills that make for successful "application".
3. The Cultural: using artistic experience to refresh and nurture Being.

My proposed "vernacular" arts education obviously offers scope in all three areas – though, as I have repeatedly said, it is through expressive participation in the cultural area that the kind of self-development I am interested in takes place. We may decide that developing an appreciation of the vernacular tradition in, say, music or drama is an important factor in raising a child's expressive level of performance. Undoubtedly children will need to be instructed in the practices of making, performing and audiencing. The curriculum as a whole will be evaluated however in terms of the quality of the children's experience, of their engagement in "vernacular" arts activities.

The traditional models and contents of the arts curriculum would need to be revised and re-aligned. For instance, no longer would music education be dominated by the classical, western repertoire – instead the spirit and to some extent the substance of contemporary popular and folk music (the music with "body" in it) would take centre-stage. Drama studies would cease to focus upon the classic texts of the past and of contemporary "high" theatre, but would explore T.V., video, film and more popular theatrical idioms. (Several modern main-stream directors have shown interest in recent years in moving their productions into the street and the market place, the meeting hall, the pub. They have also turned to more popular idioms in the making of dramatic spectacle. These important developments are little reflected in, say, O and A level drama courses). Pop music is, of course, part of a multi-media experience for the young that includes movement, dance, graphics, drama, make-up, costume. Our vernacular arts curriculum would be similarly eclectic and multi-disciplinary. It would, hopefully, have a strong cross-cultural quality as well. Arts events or happenings (collective, multi-disciplinary occasions) would be more the rule than, say, the traditional exhibitions of paintings, the annual school plays and end of year concerts. The classes would be jam sessions and the public events, community happenings. Arts lessons would generate an artistic dimension in the school's life – not merely function as yet another variation on an academic or vocational theme. There would be room for cartoon, comic strip, food, film, make-up, D.I.Y., clothing, the fair ground, musak, Boots Art, pop, electronic games, cars, bikes, hair, graffiti, advertising, entertainment, politics. The esoteric practices of the studio, the theatre, the concert hall, the gallery would be replaced by an altogether more robust, more plebeian, more ephemeral range of activities – all imbued with what I have called, the vernacular spirit.

The arts teacher will need new skills appropriate to the new curricula and the new media. He or she will need to be a craftsman of course – and that means knowing about the new media. It follows that schools will need the new media too. More challengingly I see the arts teacher as a much more enigmatic figure than we have been accustomed to. The role becomes one more in keeping with the "liminal" status and function of the vernacular arts. Arts teacher as provocateur, saboteur; as jester, fool, juggler, jongleur, troubadour, mendicant, vagabond; as guru, go-between, shaman, magician; having only "allowed" status, authority and scope; as non-impositional, non-purposive, non-strategic, impulsive, non-judgemental; as the faithful servant, entertainer, poet; scapegoat; jack-a-lantern; story-teller, bard. In all these roles the art teacher has to be "present".

"The teacher can only be present to his students if he appeals, as art does, to their freedom. He can only be present if he himself is engaged in searching and choosing, if he is committed, and if he cares. The teacher, having identified himself as a lover of art and freedom, can only offer possibility. He can only try to free his students to love in their own way. If he succeeds, if they dare to chance the jungle river and the underground and the void, there will be interior journeys taking place. There will be movements towards meaning, assertions of freedom. People will be learning to rebel". (Maxine Greene in Denton, 1974)

We need to experiment with methods and with content so as to establish a legitimate curriculum for children and young people: one for which the watch-words are participation, inter-action and spontaneity. This means, essentially, letting the media turn them on and then helping them not only to gain the appropriate knowledge and know-how, but to discover how to engage creatively with their own imaginations and sensibilities. It is this that I mean by the vernacular principle – we are talking about openness, accessibility and freedom to pursue the truth with others. These, of course, have always been the true characteristics of the arts, High and Low, Marginal and Central. I am certainly not suggesting – as was the vogue some years back – substituting, say, the music of the Beatles for the music of Beethoven, in an otherwise traditionally academic school music curriculum. I am suggesting that – whatever forms we invoke, whatever artistic styles, conventions or idioms we choose to adopt in school – the truth we are interested in has to be the children's – we must take on board what the children find truthful and valid. Their experiences of the arts in school must be authentic. Whatever undermines their commitment or defuses their concern is anathema to the pursuit of their truth, their sense of integrity.

I am also suggesting there is probably much more scope on the creative side for the utilization of popular cultural resources and practices than we have hitherto allowed in school. I find it infinitely more appropriate for instance that an O level group of drama students create a T.V.-style fantasy of their own, based upon the appeal of a surrealistic record sleeve than that they flog themselves to death trying to make something of Pinter's play *The Room*. (Why Pinter? one asks.) I am arguing for a change of heart in arts education – a change of style, not merely for a simple change of content, for the substituting of Trash Art for Posh Art, Low for High. We can surely take from whatever area, whatever culture we like – just so long as our commitment is to the principle of "design" and that the teachers ensure that their designing youngsters are making what Maxine Green in the passage just quoted calls "interior journeys". Let's not disparage what Andrew Brighton in the paper referred to in the Preface dismisses as a "paltry creativity", if creativity is what it really is. Rather a hundred successful Desmond Bagleys than a hundred failed Virginia Woolfs. My objection to the dominant ethos of the classical repertoire and of the arts commodity system in education is that they stifle spontaneity and inhibit integrity. We need of course not just to rescue the general school arts curriculum from the fate that has befallen the arts. The arts themselves – as many artists and critics are increasingly aware – need rescuing from this debilitating and emasculating process themselves. The arts, to be worthy of the name, minister to the integrity of the individual. Fudging and faking – cheating oneself – is pernicious to the soul, is a species of despair. These are the hallmarks of hopelessness. If we require of arts education, of aesthetic education, that they confirm our faith in timeless human values, in what Iris Murdoch has called "the sovereignty of good", we must begin by prizing every occasion that offers to increase the child's self-confidence and self-sufficiency as an expressive being. "If we are looking for models in the art world, we could do a lot worse than take our cue from Ed Berman's *Interaction Trust* and John Fox's *Welfare State International* (see Coult and Kershaw 1983)."

CHAPTER 6

The Poetics of Day-dream

We experience the numinous whenever, under particular conditions, we sense that in perceiving the sensuous world we are ordering or discovering coherence in our own life. The "condition" seemingly so crucial to these moments of revelation has been described by Gaston Bachelard as day-dream (see his book *The Poetics of Space*). As arts teachers we must ask ourselves how we can make such values legitimate in our classrooms when they are obviously so much at odds with the prevailing ethos. The operation of sensibility may be seen as comprising three closely related forms of perception. At the basic level sensibility identifies coherence, discerns structure. This might arguably be called the pre-aesthetic level of sensibility in which our attention has an essentially pragmatic character. True aesthetic perception occurs once we begin to take a "disinterested interest" in phenomenal structures for their own sake, and to value their essential integrity or quality. When phenomena are understood as poetic signs evocative of life values we are in the presence of art and aesthetic sensibility has achieved its most specialized form.

* * * * *

In a recently published collection of essays John Berger (1980) attempts to describe his experience observing a field.

> "Shelf of a field, green, within easy reach, the grass on it not yet high, papered with blue sky through which yellow has grown to make pure green, the surface colour of what the basin of the world contains, attendant field .... Remember what it was like to be sung to sleep. If you are fortunate, the memory will be more recent than childhood. The repeated lines of words and music are like paths .... Into the silence, which was also at times a roar, of my thoughts and questions forever returning to myself to search there for an explanation of my life and its purpose, into this concentrated tiny hub of dense silent noise, came the cackle of a hen from a nearby back garden, and at that moment that cackle, its distinct sharp-edged existence beneath a blue sky with white clouds, induced in me an intense awareness of freedom."

Berger confesses to the difficulty of capturing the experience in words. It is, somehow, ineffable he suggests, because it exists "at a level of perception and

49

feeling which is probably pre-verbal". He feels confident that, for all the difficulty of describing it or of giving it a name, the experience is, in one form or another, a common one. Any field might do "if perceived in a certain way". He goes on to specify the feature essential to the particular experience of field as the site of an action (in the dramatic sense of the pattern of events) describing how the experience asserts itself and takes possession of his attention.

> "You watch a child walking and when he has left the field deserted and eventless, you notice a cat jump down into it from the top of a wall."

He then observes that this experience takes place "outside" normal time, the narrative time of your everyday life. How does the perception of the visible field extended in space interrupt this narrative? His answer is very relevant for us:

> "You relate the events which you have seen and are still seeing to the field. It is not only the field that frames them, it also *contains* them. The existence of the field is the precondition for their occurring in the way that they have done and for the way in which others are still occurring. All events exist as definable events by virtue of their relation to other events. You have defined the events you have seen primarily but not necessarily exhaustively by relating them to the event of the field, which at the same time is literally and symbolically the *ground* of the events which are taking place within it."

Berger concludes his account by stressing its illogical and revelatory nature:

> "At first I referred to the field as a space awaiting events; now I refer to it as an event in itself. But this inconsistency parallels exactly the apparently illogical nature of the experience. Suddenly an experience of disinterested observation opens in its centre and gives birth to a happiness which is instantly recognizable as your own. The field that you are standing before appears to have the same proportions as your own life."

I have followed Berger's account carefully and presented it in detail because it offers so much to us. It is, as I am sure the reader will have recognized, a beautiful and accurate evocation of the operation of sensibility showing how, what he calls "disinterested observation" becomes a search, first of all for structure, for relatedness between one event and another, and between form and symbol, and then for personal meaning. The field eventually acts for him as a sign, as an image that evokes a happiness he immediately recognizes. The field appears as having "the same proportions" as his own life. The field is felt to correspond with, to be a correlation of, his own being.

Richard Wollheim (1979) discusses the phenomenon of "correspondence" to suggest that it entails or is an aspect of recognition. Art, according to

Wollheim, while making use of the same process of psychological projection, involves a different quality of perception. Art is not recognition but cognition – that is to say art always brings about, when it is successful, knowing: a new order of being. It is characteristically cognitive in the sense that in the experience of art we achieve knowing. Wollheim allows to ordinary perception its positive, formative, imaginative activity without equating it with the reconstituting activity of creative work in the arts. We have already discussed the different aspects of those experiences which allow us to dwell upon – perhaps it would be more accurate to say to dwell *in* – familiar sensate structure, savouring the happy flow of feeling and sensing its recreative and affirming influence upon our lives, and of those other more challenging, more problematic occasions in the course of which we possibly undergo even considerable stress and frustration as we await the insight that will give us the formula in terms of which seemingly disparate experiences may achieve relationship and, hence, significance. Berger's experience is of this sort. I am sure he is right when he says it is a "common" experience – though perhaps not common enough. We all know how difficult it is to find the time to stand and stare. And, of course, the experience will never take off for us unless we discover how to look, for Berger notes – more or less in passing – that his field had to be looked at, perceived "in a certain way". I would, in line with my own argument, want to say that the "certain way" in question is the way of sensibility: perception informed by feeling, aesthetic knowing.

Berger allows the field to reveal itself to him. He does not merely survey it – still less, look at it with the "surveyor's" pragmatic eye. It is a gratuitous act that he makes in the face of the field's *presence;* attending to it feelingly the imagination is free to go about its task of reconstituting it as "fiction". Space and time become "dramatized" – the flow of events evokes and orchestrates a complex feeling state within the watcher so that he perceives an infallible correspondence between the field and the event that he senses himself, as a person, to be. So it signals to him: become sign.

I can recall several similar occasions in my own life. One particularly memorable moment when I was walking in North Wales. I was in a lane bounded by high hedges through which I had an occasional glimpse of a wide expanse of countryside running away to a line of low, softly undulating hills. I came to a gateway and there was the prospect, framed and held in the gap between the gateposts. The recognition – of my own happiness – was instantaneous. The fields first sloped down away from me and then, rather like Berger's field, rose up gently, tilting the surface towards me. This tilted landscape ended abruptly at the low range of hills whose wavy tops formed a clear horizon across the bright sky. I "knew" there was sea beyond those hills, the sky told me so. Between the lane in which I was standing and the hills at the horizon cattle stood grazing and, in a field on the further slope, a combine-harvester was at work. The happiness I recognized was, and remains unmistakably mine, and that "vision" equally unmistakably me. I knew that place, that feeling was me. As for looking "in a certain way", all I could say about that would be that I was feeling relatively relaxed and dreamy at the time. I hadn't in the least expected such a moment but was "available", as it happened. I suspect the slow pace – I was pushing a pram – the warmth of the late summer afternoon, had induced a kind of reverie in me. But really it just happened. Never to be forgotten though and still, as Wordsworth's experience above Tintern Abbey, a source of pleasure and reassurance somehow.

I strongly suspect, along with Berger, that this kind of thing happens to people a lot: it must stand for me as a prime instance of sensibility at work, at the point where viewing becomes vision, where sight achieves significance. Which leads me to suggest that perhaps a useful way of considering that area of experience which we call "aesthetic" would be as a continuum that extends across the whole range of human experience from the most pragmatic or transactional to the most visionary or poetic. But even as I say that, and useful though the idea of a continuum might be, I sense that there is something about the linear, two dimensional character of that concept which leaves me dissatisfied. I want rather, I think, to invoke the dimension of depth and to see the aesthetic as having levels of meaning, and sensibility operating as a kind of spiral staircase reaching and carrying the perceiver from layer to layer, from level to level, with the pragmatic and transactional at the surface and the poetic sign hidden beyond, in the depth of its experience. This would prevent my drawing any kind of dividing line across the aesthetic separating one experience from another; rather we should have to concede that all our experiences of coherence may be responded to more or less superficially, in aesthetic terms. So "sign" would function as a kind of deeper, more profound level of perception, possible in respect of any phenomenon and more likely in respect of some than of others. And, to get back to Berger's field, the "certain way" he refers to would simply be a readiness and ability to sink into, be drawn into a deeper level of awareness than might, for example, be appropriate if one were viewing the acreage as so much real-estate. Berger's interest was "disinterested" – and in terms of my three-dimensional model, his sensibility, as with my own experience, was already at level two or beyond. It had moved immediately to that already deeper than surface level by virtue of the circumstances attending this particular experience.

> "This field affords me considerable pleasure. Why then do I not sometimes walk here – it is quite near my flat – instead of relying on being stopped there by the closed level crossing? It is a question of contingencies overlapping. The events which take place in the field – two birds chasing one another, a cloud crossing the sun and changing the colour of the green – acquire a special significance because they occur during the minute or two during which I am obliged to wait. It is as

though these minutes fill a certain area of time which exactly fits the spacial area of the field. Time and space conjoin."

Being in a car for any length of time invariably induces this frame of mind in me. In Berger's case the enforced nature of the interlude at the closed level crossing has all the makings of "boundary" awareness we discussed in Chapter 2. We seem to be saying that for the deeper levels of sensibility to be engaged we must, by one means or another, achieve a break with, or breach the membrane of pragmatic, everyday awareness and attention. This attention itself must be altered in its mode of operation, be "framed".

This links up, I think, with Ehrenzweig's (1967) notion of de-focusing, of scanning, of what he calls "de-differentiation" in which imagination roams swiftly and freely across the information field, creating congruences and coherences of an order quite different from that required by our more habitual, more mundane transactions. We might not want to speak of the state of trance in this connection, though we may feel we are and seem to be entranced. Reverie or day-dreaming are possibly less threatening ideas, but as we have seen, all partake of the idea that we stand open, receptive before the object (pattern or structure) and admit it – allow it to take possession of us. Just as we do when listening to music or watching a play in the theatre. I always marvel at the way "parties" are conducted round art galleries – like people at an identity parade or leafing through criminal records. One picture at a time is enough for me and I settle down and lose myself – for as long as the security people can contain their natural suspicion in the face of such odd behaviour.

If day-dream is the necessary condition of deep sensibility, it is so whether sensibility is operative in the making or receiving processes. And perhaps it would be hard to say of any manifestation of sensibility, even at its supposedly most transactional level, that there is absolutely no detachment, no abstraction of mind in order to attend in that "certain way". Persig's (1976) memorable and influential book *Zen and the Art of Motorcycle Maintenance* is about sensibility above everything else: its concern with Quality is precisely this surrendering of mind to feeling as a way of knowing, and maintaining his persecuted motorbike becomes at once a vital piece of transaction in the world and a sacrament: a sign. Sensibility is at work whenever we order experience on the basis of sensuous criteria – which leaves every aspect of our transactions with the material and the imaginary world open to its influence.

By the same token our lives are impoverished, our sensibility downgraded, as occasions of sensuous forming dry up. We might consider the working days of the computer-programmer, the bank clerk, the super-market cashier, the copy-typist, the assembly-line "hand", the academic, the convenience-food dispenser, at home or in the high-street. Work that reduces formative contact with materials, that is but the extension of a largely mechanical process, that requires only the interpretation of abstractions (as, for instance, in the assembly of packaged furniture) by denying the occasion for direct interaction with sensuous forms and any need or opportunity for acting decisively and personally in respect of them, is a denial and an erosion of sensibility. It seems reasonable to assume that, unpractised, the skills of sensibility will not only fail to develop but will actually deteriorate. Which is perhaps why there will always be some sense in seeing the arts as the subjects within the curriculum most likely to have aesthetic outcomes, not simply because, in the popular mind the terms aesthetics and art are interchangeable but in the sense that the arts are committed more than perhaps any other subject – including such subjects as craft-design-technology – to the significant exploitation and ordering of sensuous materials. Whereas, of course, it would be difficult to discover amongst any of the other subject areas, with very few exceptions, any exercise of sensibility at all. If sensibility is the exercise of sensuous judgement you find little or no evidence of it in the child's secondary school experience of maths or science, the humanities or languages. Words, for instance, are treated more or less entirely as discursive symbols in English and when structure and order become teaching points, convention rather than impulse is invoked as the central principle. Which is another way of saying that the so-called creative approach to writing and to literary appreciation is still a minority interest among English teachers and brings virtually no reward at the level of the public examination.

Of course there are subjects other than the arts where sensibility plays some part and might indeed play a considerable part. The ordering of materials according to an emergent sense of quality would seem to be required of all craft activities for instance, whether we are talking of the shaving of wood, the manipulation of metals and plastics, the making of food, the design and creation of fabrics and textiles. New courses in physical education – when not geared too obsessively to the bizarre requirements of competitive gymnastics – also stress response to materials, in this instance, response to the materiality of one's own body and the bodies of others. The dilemma of many craft teachers, however, as I see it, is that if they are to be fully contemporary, not simply in design but in process, they risk the surrender of much in the child's experience that would exercise and enhance sensibility; whereas if they stick to the old ways, to hand-work, to training touch, feel, eye, they can all too easily fall into the nostalgic trap of the cultural conservationist whose work acquires inevitably more and more of a curiosity designation. And I am the last person to be able to advise them how to resolve the problem. It is an acute one nevertheless and the only prospect of a way through seems to lie in the work of those teachers who have chosen to give their teaching a creative and expressive bias – i.e. to move it away from the fabrication of tools, ornaments and functional objects and towards those artifacts Margolis writes of, the principal interest of which lies in their "design". All making from diagrams, all fitting (as garage mechanics these days are required more and more merely to "fit" sealed units, rather than to repair, remake or refashion the machine), all mere conceptual abstraction, will be anathema to such teachers. The current trend in design education towards the mental problem-solving approach realized in designs that are subject to trial and error testing, is so much at one with the rest of the academic conceptualizing curriculum as to be more or less entirely at odds with the aesthetic principle that I am trying to develop.

Anyone interested in the notion of general aesthetic education is bound to regret the progressive de-sensualizing of the curriculum as a whole and to look for whatever occasion offers for the re-introduction of some scope for sensibility. For occasions of qualitative judgement making. Our infant and primary schools are still relatively unregenerate: occasions for direct sensing, for qualitative decisions, for the imaginative integration of sensuous elements, are still to be found throughout the child's day. But the natural tendency for the secondary school child to rely increasingly upon discursive rather than presentational symbols for the handling of feelings and ideas meets an essentially academically oriented system which is all too eager to capitalize on this tendency and to set the adolescent's education running upon a purely rational track. Art of course operates quite differently in regard to symbolic function. As we have seen, Louis Arnaud Reid emphasizes the materiality, the direct sensuous impact of art as symbol, in his phrase "meaning embodied". It is in embodiment – it is in the materiality and body of the artwork, that its meaning is presented, and we apprehend that meaning directly, through the senses operating upon imagination, not by the processes of abstract thought. Aesthetic education requires, among other things – and, as we shall see, there are other things – the development and refinement of sensibility through the exercise of qualitative judgement. Judgements in the pragmatic field tend to be quantitative; in the aesthetic field they are qualitative. By which we mean they are concerned with the way in which and with the extent to which a given structure achieves coherence in its own terms. The sciences quantify; the arts qualify.

However, as Raymond Williams (1976) pointed out, the term art was once applied to all skills and all fields of knowledge. Science itself was "an art". Whatever the reasons may be, one of the consequences of industrial and technological progress has been the erosion of the processes of imagination and sensibility in, for example, the field of medicine. As medicine has become high technology, nursing (and doctoring and surgery) have lapsed into machine tending and machine programming. Modern life seems to be throwing up more and more symptoms of alienated, repressed and frustrated human beings at the very time when the availability of sympathetic human beings "called" to the profession of healing seems about to collapse. All we have to offer as an alternative is the "stabilized medication programme" and the electric shock. It is hard to imagine another field of work that makes such critical demands upon sensibility and which is quite so disastrously affected by its demise at all levels of the profession.

Arguably the teacher – the "good-enough teacher" (Ross, 1978) – is almost as dependent upon sensibility as the doctor and the therapist. It is certainly hard to appreciate how any teacher can create the kind of circumstances in which the child feels free to learn, without exercising sensibility, intelligent feeling, in monitoring the child's readiness and achievement, needs and competences. I would suspect we need science, maths and language teachers, every bit as "sensible" as their arts colleagues are expected to be. And the teaching of these non-arts subjects should be examined for whatever occasions might be embedded in them for the deployment and development of the sensibilities of the children. Occasions should be sought and exploited in which the perception of significant form is given every encouragement in the practice of science, maths and language learning. In which what constitutes quality – as coherent form – is examined, extolled and apprehended. All qualitative judgements are inherently aesthetic and sensibility is an indispensable dimension of human action, potentially as critical in science as in art. The "visionary" writings of scientists such as Michael Polanyi, Gaston Bachelard, John Young, Gregory Bateson, Jacob Bronowski, are surely testimony enough. To identify aesthetic education with the arts is both conceptually inexact and philosophically wrong. The aesthetic is a genuinely cross-curricular dimension of education.

As I have said already in attempting to conceptualize the operation of sensibility, I think we may be better off with a three-dimensional spiral than a linear scale. Our analysis so far would seem to suggest that there might be three levels of conscious operation. *The surface level would be what I want to call the level of pragmatic attachment* – it might be better to describe this level as pre-aesthetic rather than achieving full aesthetic status. We are attending to sensuous data with a claim already made upon and admitted by our mental and motor performance. This is the level of the purely pragmatic: we have a practical outcome in mind that is directly linked with such central life issues as security, love, status, nourishment, livelihood, communication, efficiency. Here our sense of what fits, of the connection between this phenomenon and that, is largely determined by operational or pragmatic constraints. Indeed the operation of sensibility at this "first" level is quite emphatically constrained or "interested" – which is in a sense precisely what I mean by my term, attached.

The deeper and richer levels of sensibility are characterized by increasing disinterestedness: so the next threshold in our spiral, descending model, is the threshold of attentional detachment. Which means that even when mending your motorbike or making up the fire or decorating a room or preparing a meal, for all that each of these is an activity that is radically tied to the production of an end result which will be tested by quite stringent and quite objective criteria, nonetheless they all admit of an element, a degree of detachment which allows some measure of freedom to the play of sensibility. For example there is motorcycle maintenance, fire tending, interior decorating and cooking that are predominantly functionalist in orientation, and there are the same tasks which may be lent a certain value as artifacts in their own right almost, and of which we desire that they manifest some inherent principle or quality to advantage. Undoubtedly such attention will be closely tied up with the actual effectiveness of the finished work, but we recognise, in the word "finish" itself, some intrinsic interest or quality that attends and affects our appraisal of a piece of work over and above its functional performance. It is as if the thing made its own demands of us, the maker, to see it right, to present it at its best. It betokens an in-built sense of the inherent value and dignity of things made and done. Almost a respectfulness towards them. So disinterestedness, which can be a kind of painstaking and restraint, a kind of self-denial on the part of the maker, becomes one of the hall-marks of aesthetic sensibility.

Self-denial is of course the opposite of self-indulgence, self-assertion, and we shall want to insist, I think, that a self-denying stance before experience is one of the critical aesthetic virtues. At the level of disinterestedness we are prepared to grant the object of perception a uniqueness of being, an identity claiming our respect. *We have moved from the perception of qualities to a recognition of quality.* We become attentive to the thing itself rather than to its function, its utility. Being aware of it in its own right means being able to formulate, no matter how intuitively, the principle of its coherence in the world, and so, to respect and minister to its uniqueness, its integrity. Given this emergent awareness of the thing itself we become sensitive to its authenticity, to its genuineness. There is something radically disqualifying in the discovery of whatever is false, phoney, dishonest or inauthentic in an object which we are prepared to credit with an identity of its own, a structure worthy of our respect. Once we are prepared to grant our respect we demand consistency, constancy, faithfulness: all those qualities we similarly require of people. Aesthetic perception at this "second" level has clearly moved a long way from the pragmatic criteria which take prior claim at the transactional or pre-aesthetic level.

Our third, and ultimate level of sensibility allows for the possibility of expression and the emergence of sign. Beyond the disinterested respect for the thing itself lies the possibility of its coming to signify other than itself – and yet not lose its own identity. This is the level of metaphor, the level of the expressive character of the sensuous, the power latent in all sensuous phenomena to arouse and organize feeling idea. At this level we experience an even greater access of disinterestedness as we become aware of a certain openness or multi-dimensionality of meaning in the form we have described. This is clearly the level of imaginative feeling, the level at which it becomes not simply possible but inevitable that we discern "correspondence" between our own life and the "life" or "presence" of the "character" of the object that confronts us and asserts its influence upon us. Here we may recall John Berger's "field". It is also the level of artistic projection, of that creativity which ordains that material phenomena should feature as signs in the world – that we can abstract to ourselves meanings embodied in the signs we make and thereby achieve new levels of affective coherence. I have decided to use the word "tacit" to describe this third level of attention, with its connotations of meaning reserved or implicit, of silence and stillness (from the latin "tacere"). This third level is the level of latent or potential meaning, of meaning awaiting realization, of connections to be made, truths to be revealed. The realm, as I have said of metaphor, of sign. It is *the poetic dimension of aesthetic experience.*

So my model of "sensible" operations reaches its ultimate level and yet I am tempted to add a further feature to it. And that would be a spiral operating in the opposite direction and rising to coincide with the descending spiral at level three. The descending spiral becomes consciousness and the ascending spiral, spirit or unconsciousness. If there are comparable levels in the unconscious spiral they would simply be the pure unconscious – that level beyond all knowing – and the pre-conscious of which we are at times dimly, intuitively aware and which, at least to a limited extent, we seem able to influence and evoke. Engagement, interaction, between conscious and unconscious processes can then be posited at the third level of sensibility or of aesthetic perception, at the level of what I call "tacit" operations.

If such a model of "sensible" action is permitted it will be seen that it is constituted at least at the third level, of both conscious and unconscious processes. My suspicion is that for the model to be useful we need to sense the spiral movement of consciousness as in constant ebb and flow – at least when not suffering under constraint or inhibition – although it suggests discrete kinds of response associated with different levels of operation, in practice the pragmatic will be felt at the deep level of sign, and the tacit, as one would expect, at least implicit at the level of surface. We are probably, as with the discarded linear scale, speaking of degrees of influence in respect of any one particular experience. The model does serve nevertheless to demonstrate my own conception of the homogeneity of the aesthetic with the artistic whilst at the same time rendering the arts as a special and separate manifestation of the aesthetic. It might for instance help us to distinguish those aesthetic criteria which would have immediate relevance for all subjects in the curriculum, namely Level 2 (Quality), from those of special relevance to the arts, namely at Level 3 (Tacit Operations). Works of art are subject to all criteria in as much as all art is aesthetic; on the other hand we can quite properly grant an aesthetic dimension to the assessment of scientific, technical and mathematical forms for instance without having to make nonsense of our definition of art and say that they too must be art. Art and aesthetics are not synonymous. They can be usefully and logically separated. But neither are they so disconnected, so dissociated that it makes sense to abandon the term aesthetic as having no function simply because all aesthetic criteria are subsumed within what we mean by art. I would want to maintain that we can and indeed should speak of the Aesthetic Dimension of Education without being understood as meaning simply the practice of the creative arts, still less the appreciation of High Art.

I have tried to show that all subjects have an aesthetic dimension – manifest at Level 2 of the model and with some connection at Level 3 – and I want to suggest that it behoves all teachers of whatever subject in all schools at whatever level to consider the aesthetic dimension of their work, since the education of sensibility is a vital responsibility shared by us all. It cannot be left to the arts people who have their own special commitment to Level 3 and to the process of "signing" by correspondence and expression. The Tacit is the realm of the artistic and is governed by two active principles: creativity and imagination. It is the region of stillness, silence, wordlessness – of that which is not yet. We shall clearly want to look at what happens at Level 3 in some detail, for this essay, despite its general concerns with the aesthetic dimension as a factor of the whole curriculum is, nevertheless, specially committed to appraise and, hopefully shed some light upon the possibility of a new emphasis in creative arts education. But before proceeding to do so I want to linger just a little longer over these more general matters.

CHAPTER 7

Cordiality

In the pre-industrial past there was a quality about adult working life that gave real scope to every man's capacity for disinterested interest. Life itself had an organic, integrated quality, despite hardships and privations, which allowed free play to the operation of sensibility. The industrial revolution and its outcomes have eroded our occasions for sensible action and the electronic revolution that followed has reduced still further men's opportunities to express themselves through their work. However, sensible action is the heart of the aesthetic curriculum and we can learn a lot about what we might be doing in schools from looking at the lives of men and women more closely in touch with the faculty of feeling than is perhaps usual nowadays. If we ask ourselves, "What's the use of aesthetics in education?" we could do a lot worse than answer "To refresh and restore the vital spirit". Cordiality is an inveterate outcome of any truly aesthetic experience. Creating the conditions of cordiality is perhaps our prime task in arts education; making a satisfactory life our ultimate objective.

★　★　★　★　★

If sensibility is that faculty or capacity of the human mind charged among other things with the responsibility of creating psychic order, of helping us to come to terms with and mature in respect of our feelings, then it is clearly of central importance in education, and centrally important to all educators. The current official endorsement of the back-to-basics mentality in education is such an instance of acute, political short-sightedness for there is clearly a sense in which the education of feeling, imagination, creativity, the sense of personal worth, the feeling for quality, were never more urgently needed. All those features of subjective experience that in their turn affect not just the quality of our actions but our very capacity, our inclination to act at all, our motives for acting intelligently and intelligibly in the world. Schools have always been places slow to change, slow to respond to social need; have always been hide-bound by ignorance and institutionalized forms of neglect. And by the same token there have always been, and mercifully continue to be, the exceptions: invariably schools run upon humanistic principles that have given due weight to the sacramental. I want to match the illustration from John Berger's writings with another instance of aesthetic perception, of sensibility at work, which I came across recently. If Berger's experience could reasonably be called a "common" one, this next illustration was perhaps a good deal commoner in days gone by than it is now.

H.J. Massingham (1939) gives a beautifully evocative account of the work of the traditional "bodger". A bodger makes chairs: is a wood-turner; this traditional craft was particularly practised in the Chiltern Hills and there the bodgers would set up their temporary "hovels" amidst the beech woods and for miserly rewards produce the quality of chair leg now only to be found in seventeenth-century antiques. Massingham knew one such bodger well and spent many hours talking with him and watching him at work amidst the wood-shavings. His name was Samuel Rockall of Turville Heath.

> "The true craftsman controls and executes all the processes of his craft from raw originals to the finished product, no matter how many they be. He is thus divided by a cleavage absolute from the one-man-one-bolt system of modern, minutely subdivided industry. That is why the rural master-man remains by the law of his being close to nature. He is not merely surrounded by nature; he not only takes his tools and materials from nature, but he repeats the ordered unfoldings of nature from the seed to the flower, from the grain to the ear, from alpha to omega. This is the secret of good craftsmanship and the condition of its blossoming, that the man shall take the fruits of the earth from the hands of nature, and with his own hands transform them into the final form he destines for them, to be at once useful for the needs of his fellows and pleasurable to their eyes. From tree to mast: it is the same thing over and again but on a new turn of the spiral of creation. Samuel Rockall buys and axes his own trees where they stand in the woodland, and so his craft is organic. He conducts all the operations from the tree in the forest to the chair by the fire, and like a magician wills nature to come out of the weather into the home."

I cite this passage, and its portrait of the old wood bodger, not in any spirit of nostalgia – though I am pleasantly and a little sadly reminded of many such old men as I have known in my own time: my own Uncle Sam, village storekeeper-cum-doctor, hedge-drashers, carters, blacksmiths, iron workers, and their women folk too who toiled away as young maids "in service". What is so striking in Massingham's record is the richness, the "wholeness" of the old man's working experience. No doubt he cursed the cold and the mud to say nothing of the poor rewards his efforts won him. Nevertheless everything about his work, its over-arching rhythms, the close ties with the natural calendar, speed without hurry, time to give his own special rendering to what were essentially unchanging forms – all those characteristics of his life that created the "conditions" in which his craft blossomed and flourished. His skills of eye, hand and judgement; his dexterity, strength and immense know-how.

You might hope that despite the rigours of living by such means, the old man's character might reflect some of the virtues of his work, and if Massingham is to be believed, you would not be disappointed. The bodger had tried working behind the power-lathe in High Wycombe as an "improver" but had given it up after five months. "I felt shut in", he said "like a bird that's put in a cage" – and, given the open and independent life he was used to, well he might.

> "Certainly the bodgers – Samuel Rockall is not the least representative because he is *primus-inter-pares* – are happy men. They are open, courteous in their independence, quiet and assured in the midst of their arduous labours and the rigours of their heavy, consistent output. They seem very old-fashioned because their peace is unknown to the age they live in, their content an anachronism."

These were men in whose lives the aesthetic was the unacknowledged keystone. Sensibility informed their work and was radiant in their personalities. It was, of course, a robust sensibility – there was nothing precious, effete or self-conscious about it, and yet the marriage between head and hand was absolute and abiding: eyes, backs, legs, fingers were all highly trained, highly "intelligent", and the results of their work had to meet criteria of effectiveness and of finish: the turned wood must do the job it was intended for, there must be an essential congruence or concord between materials and function, but also, and equally importantly, the work had to have the right feel, had to look good. No fudging, no cheating, no skimping. We all know the pleasure to be had from something that not only does its job well but feels and looks good too. There is a kind of virtue, a strength almost that invigorates the object – so we take the kind of pleasure in it that we take in watching a healthy child or animal. Objects too can be imbued with a vital spirit, a beauty that emanates from the heart or the soul of the thing and it is not simply a matter of appearance, of decoration or of polish. I was chopping kindling wood the other day and discovered that the "off-cut" I was endeavouring to split was badly twisted. The sawmill had completely disregarded the natural movement of the timber and cut across its pattern of growth so as to produce a section that for all its apparent uniformity would never be truly serviceable. It was a "painful" sight that distorted and abused stump! As for splitting it – I just had to give up.

Making good things, "compleat" things with a distinct "virtue" or strength or spirit of their own, rubs off on you so it would seem – much as a life-time working over a potter's wheel seems to leave you with an ineradicable wobble of the head as if it had become, over the years, a slightly unbalanced vessel itself. The whole business of trying to assess the possible good of doing certain things in school – like saying that learning poetry or Latin is good for character building, or drama good for self-confidence – is a very awkward topic I feel. It seems relatively uncontroversial to assert that learning maths is good for counting, and doing PE good for vaulting and somersaulting. Even history is good for dates and English good for spelling – well, it used to be. But when someone says "What's the use of weaving, Miss?" and you know that they're not intending weavers, it's a bit hard to say what weaving's good for without resorting to the standard fall-back position of saying "Well you just do it because I think it's good for you". The things children do in school are supposed – it is popularly imagined – to be doing them some good. To be good for something. And it is not only the children who feel that perhaps some things required of them are good for nothing very much – or for precious little. Bodging must have been good for making a living once upon a time – and if not particularly good for that purpose, at least good enough.

What could you begin to say that the arts were good for – inside or outside school? Some would even reckon it to be an unfair question. What is the *good* of aesthetic education? What is the *good* of sensibility? These are awkward questions to deal with as I say, and the reason is probably because what people are really asking is "What's the *use* of art, aesthetics, sensibility and so forth?" And by use they have in mind something strictly pragmatic. Can you sell it, trade or cash it in, get credit on the strength of it, get something done with it? But even if we are allowed that such particular "uses" cannot reasonably be applied to all the things people rightly value in life – like having children, like friendship, like playing games, making love and so forth – we still expect that time spent on learning things in school should be good for something: like good for helping you to get on with other people, or get over your shyness, or for being a parent yourself one day, or understanding why things happen in the world. Children recognize the long-term value of such things and arts educators have been coming up with plausible answers in this vein for some time. But some scepticism surrounds these claims and demonstrating the effectiveness of arts teaching in terms of them can prove inordinately more difficult for instance than showing whether the student has acquired certain factual knowledge or practical skills in a particular field, e.g. music, drama or art. Where no occupational take-up is in question, to have become in some sense an accomplished actor or painter or composer at school is not held to be a somehow self-evidently valuable achievement. People ask "So what?" And we are back with the question, "What's sensibility *good* for?" – assuming, that is, that we know what we mean by sensibility in the first place. George Steiner (1969) has cast doubt upon the traditional claim of Eng. Lit. teachers, following Matthew Arnold, that book study would have a civilizing influence upon young gentlemen. Steiner sees no evidence of this. The tie up between English studies as moral development (embodied in the equation: literary discrimination = moral enlightenment) and the tradition of exposing the malevolence of the media, is very resilient indeed however, and such connections abound in writings about English teaching. As I have already indicated, drama is only slightly less committed to the "civilizing" programme, and resounds to all kinds of claims to moral and social rectitude and improvement. Art and music have been rather less inclined to explain themselves in these terms, still less to offer the "artist" as a model of social adjustment, for reasons that are presumably all too obvious. Music is such a highly-specialized skill it seems pointless to consider explaining music's usefulness other than by reference to the world of music. It is customary to give no explanation whatever, other than asserting that music, like Guinness, is good for you. And perhaps that's right. The arts, like Guinness, are felt somehow to be good for you even if they aren't guaranteed to make you a saint.

Whilst I was asleep one night in the course of writing this book the word "cordial" came into my mind – as a way of explaining how an aesthetic experience works upon us. My dream seemed to be saying that sensibility – the appraisal of sensuous form – was not a thought process. It was a way of availing oneself of the cordial virtue of the phenomenal object. I remembered, or half remembered, Leontes in Shakespeare's *A Winter's Tale* using the word. My sleeping mind told me that "cordial" was related to "coeur" and signified the heart as the source and centre of human feeling. Upon waking I was able to confirm this in the dictionary, which had more that was very much to the point to offer me.

> "1. Of or belonging to the heart – 1646. 2. Stimulating, comforting, or invigorating the heart; reviving, cheering – 1471. Also fig. 3. Hearty; heartfelt; sincere, genuine, warm. 1477" (SOED)

There is also a connection between what mediaeval physiologists called the "cordial spirits" and the Vital Spirits, for "the Vital Spirit resides in the heart". I found all this exciting and timely. My unconscious had done good work.

I am tempted to say that, whether successful in this respect or not, the function of sensibility is to invigorate, stimulate and comfort our vital spirits; to turn our bodies, minds and spirits towards life itself, towards living as an intrinsically valuable experience. Reviving and cheering us. Aesthetic experience is cordial to our being and whatever other characteristics might be held to define it, cordiality (warmth of feeling, heartfeltness) will perhaps be its most active principle. All this fits very well with other insights into the significance as distinct from the nature of aesthetic experience; for example, when we use the term an-aesthetic (or an-aesthetized) we mean a kind of numbing of sensibility, a freezing of the faculties of perception so that we feel neither pain nor pleasure, are rendered unconscious, unaware, in some respects dead. Certainly we live unable to respond to any stimulus, any comfort, any cheer. If to be anaesthetized is to be turned away from life, to have our sensibility rendered inoperative, then to be "aesthetized" is to be turned towards life, to be attuned to our living processes as inveterately positive and good. Biologists speak of living systems as incapable of inherently harbouring and so of generating, negative, anti-life responses within themselves. Which perhaps explains why when healthy we tend to see life as good and as a positive experience. No matter what philosophical problems such a view might pose I feel I must claim at least this for the aesthetic dimension of experience – and so, by implication, for the arts: *the function of sensibility is cordial, its end is life-enhancement.*

If you ask me what are the arts for, what is the good or the use of sensibility, I can only answer that they exist to make us feel good to be alive. Which is not quite the same thing as saying, simply, "to make us feel good", and of course it isn't the same thing at all as saying "to make us do what is good". I don't propose to allow myself to get drawn into the controversy about art and either the pleasure or the moral principles – at least not too deeply. It is clearly not enough to say that art affords pleasure, because so many other experiences afford pleasure, and there are many different kinds of pleasure anyway. I have said "feel good to be alive" – and I mean, feel good about living, about our own lives. Which would imply that art fails if, in some sense it can be said to make us feel like giving up, like despairing. It may horrify, disturb and distress us – i.e. it may not in any obvious sense cheer us up – yet its ultimate impact will be invariably positive and life-enhancing. Art will always stimulate, comfort and refresh "the heart"; *the aesthetic is essentially committed to cordiality.* It is not, even at my proposed level 1 (i.e. at the level of the discernment of structural coherence), merely a value-free function of sensing, of perceptual discernment. Aesthetic behaviour, if not exactly moral behaviour, is committed to the life-principle, the élan vital. Sensibility is the manifestation of the "cordial spirit" at work: it is intimately linked to the whole apparatus of feeling and in particular serves to stimulate all purposeful action in the world. And like every other system at work within us it is constantly renewing itself and enlarging its scope: aesthetic development in some respects is synonymous with the quality of cordiality in the sense that we would interpret all signs of affective decline, of rejection, of withdrawal, no matter what the cause, as signs of a, hopefully temporary, breakdown of sensibility. Which is why aesthetic education is not simply a question of training in practical or discriminatory skills, it is crucially tied into our system of values. A good aesthetic education, a healthy aesthetic development, will, by definition, increase the life-force, empower the life-drive, release all our instincts to savour life and live life to the full. It will be strengthening – virtuous. Which is perhaps why we would expect to find the twin notions of spontaneity and imagination associated with the deepest and richest levels of aesthetic experience. But we must recognize that it is not as simple as that – if the life-spirit burns fiercely it is also beset on every side by the perhaps more powerful forces of death. Actual death will always "put out the light". So life becomes a gesture of impudent defiance in the face of a consuming chaos, darkness and annihilation. As we reflect upon that fact in our human way we sense its special poignancy – and we make much if not most of our art out of that sense of the poignancy of human being. Art itself becomes an analogous gesture of defiance. But the aesthetic life – a tautology now since we are inclined to equate the aesthetic with the life-force itself – is threatened by all those lesser deaths that pre-figure the final curtain fall. I mean those assaults upon human freedom and dignity, everything that cages a man or a child, that turns him against himself, that renders life routine, habitual, deceitful. That denies him access to his own experience or twists and negates the primal values of truth, justice, compassion, love.

What Samuel Rockall had, despite his undoubted hardships and deprivations, was "life abundant". Massingham quotes Blake: "Exuberance is all". Wordsworth was fond of using the term "glee" in respect of those, usually rather odd, even "lunatic" souls, who seemed to him to exemplify the vital spirit. His intuition seems to have led him to place them in his own Border Country. "Euphoria" has these days perhaps rather too much of the sense of recklessness about it to be very readily used in connection with the life spirit and yet to experience that spirit is certainly to be lifted beyond the state of simply feeling well – beyond the tactful apperception of what fits. I wonder whether we don't in fact, quite rightly expect – of art certainly, if not actually of all aesthetic experiences that go beyond the simple discernment of good form – to feel euphoric!

Massingham spoke of the "conditions" in which the bodger's craftsmanship blossomed. I have come increasingly to think myself that attending to the *conditions* of the aesthetic experience, guaranteeing the conditions in which sensibility might flourish, is one of the arts teacher's principal responsibilities in a school. I am saying that among our ambitions as arts teachers we need this commitment to supply the right conditions, which is not to say that matters may rest there. I hope to be suggesting an account of the arts teacher's practices which will be both highly skilled and highly specialized. Attending to the right conditions however would be one aspect of the teacher's work – one that would in itself make very considerable demands upon the teacher. We should give more time to thinking about and supplying the *climate* that will allow the natural development of sensibility. Such a view reflects my intuition that sensibility develops individually and, even in the optimum conditions, at its own pace. That any hint of "forcing" is inherently a threat to a process which is already encoded in and prepared for in the individual's aesthetic make-up. That since we want to identify sensibility with the vital force and with natural rhythms we ought to try to be consistent in the provision, in the circumstances attending such development.

The "right conditions" for Samuel Rockall were a life lived close to nature; an organic relationship between design and achievement; personal involvement in and identification with his productive actions; a good supply of suitable materials and a deep interest in and feeling for those materials; a good supply of the right tools and skill in maintaining (even producing) them; an attitude of mind that married productivity with quality; scope for personal expression within an ancient tradition; freedom to choose to work in a particular way and to set his own standards; freedom to be the best judge of his own work; available outlets and, at least in some measure, adequate "rewards"; confidence in himself as a craftsman and content with himself as a worthwhile human being; sensibility; resourcefulness; tenacity; courage; loving-kindness; cheerfulness; exuberance; cordiality. We might fairly say that all these were "conditional" factors: they were the conditions that allowed him to attain that high level of being – you wouldn't want to speak of it in less thorough-going terms – that was so clearly his true and abiding achievement as a craftsman.

Now for a teacher to promise any child such a set of conditions in which to develop his or her sensibility might well be thought to be to promise a good deal more than he could possibly expect to deliver. But I do propose some such itinerary – relying upon "nature" to repay the teacher's efforts ten-fold. I suspect that as some of what we shall come to specify as the essential pre-conditions of the development of sensibility are supplied, the child will release and display almost undreamed of resources, as the sheath that enshrouds each new frond of a palm suddenly splits to release a beautifully enfolded fan. There is indeed a "force that through the green fuse breaks" – and I believe it not to be a brute force but a highly intelligent force more than capable of finding its own space and light, of coming to full maturity by its own divining. What is more I suspect the process of sensible development is invariant in as much that adults suddenly released through the supply of right conditions will pass, albeit more swiftly, through precisely those stages that we can identify in the development of the child. (Which is not to say that such an adult will ever fully recover from the barren years of denial, frustration and inhibition that preceded his or her eventual aesthetic release.) In aesthetic, as in all aspects of education, the right conditions will release a powerful and natural drive to grow – such a natural process of unfolding is the teacher's greatest resource. I trust in it absolutely. However I recognize that even in the realm of feeling and the arts it is not enough. I cannot really agree with Louis Arnaud Reid (Ross 1982) that if we leave them alone they will, like sheep, find their own way home. Aesthetic education is good for feeling that life is worth living. But to be good for that the child's sensibility must be freed, must be protected from whatever in its life in school and its life out of school, would inhibit, brutalize or intimidate sensibility. All that deals death and despair. Not all that is offensive and threatening, for life must give rise to such challenges and, indeed, assert itself despite and over them. There must be no sentimentalizing, no trivializing. But no dismembering and no exploiting and no prostituting of the child either.

Supplying the conditions of freedom becomes the teacher's first responsibility – making possible at least those most critical elements of the life of Samuel Rockall for every child in every school. I won't repeat them now though we shall be coming back to them. Sensibility, as we have seen, is closely associated with imagination, and I am convinced that imagination grows by having the freedom to grow. You only have to try to have a quiet meal in my house with my two sons aged four and three, to know that the child's imaginative development waits on nothing and no one. It is no good saying "No toys at the table". Everything is a toy. The long, dream-entranced sleep leaves them with a pent-up imagination that makes breakfast an appalling occasion if you can't actually go with it. Short of invoking ultimate sanctions there is no hope of keeping imagination down. The table, before you know it, has become some kind of a mechanical moon-buggy and we are all required to "pedal" like fury to avoid a disaster that is clear enough to them, despite my pleading that they eat up their cornflakes because ... because ..., though of course, quite obscure to me. They are not being either clever, or naughty, or wilful. They seem to have no power to bottle up or suppress the vivacious drive to imagine, to act playfully and expressively. And what goes for imagination goes surely for sensibility too. You can't keep a good (i.e. a healthy) child's sensibility down. Any more than a concrete path will for long keep a crocus or a blade of grass down. Such force! And such knowing, such intelligence. Presumably such greediness, such need! You can I suppose pile on the concrete so thick that it could never break through, or just resort to rooting the thing up – but those are about the only options open to you. Give it a hint, a whiff of freedom and there it is – sensible, awake, making its mark.

The anatomist, J.Z. Young (1980) cites Richard Wollheim: "A good environment is not a luxury, it is a necessity". In writing about good conditions I mean environment both in the narrow and broad senses: the ambience and the quality of the school, neighbourhood or home, as good places, and the curricular environment – the experiences set up by the teacher. Young himself warns against damage to and the deterioration of what he calls the "reward centres" of the brain:

> "If the reward centres are not working then even the most refined cultural or religious programs act in vain. The individual becomes unhappy and depressed, useless to himself and others and, ultimately, suicidal". (Page 140)

Here, to my mind, is exactly the picture of the person whose aesthetic powers have become corrupted or inoperative. His condition is the precise opposite of cordiality. Young suggests that what I call sensibility gives rise to the whole symbolic system of man's values and beliefs, encoded as religion and as the arts. "They are not merely peripheral, luxury activities", he writes. "They are literally the most important of all the functional features that ensure human homeostasis". For Young, as for me, the operation of sensibility is basic to the discernment of structure and meaning in life-events, as it is to the embodiment of meaning in the arts:

> "The activities that go to the creation and enjoyment of works of art are thus quintessentially those by which the brain, working every day as a creative agent, synthesizes input from the world to make a satisfactory life." (Page 233)

CHAPTER 8

The Whole and the Holy

What are the conditions of cordiality? Clearly we have to equip children with particular skills, bring out a range of latent abilities, help them to experience and understand, help them to self-sufficiency in their sensible actions – we have to see that their personal resources are adequate, their sensibilities qualified. Circumstances also materially affect the flowering of sensibility – the schools must offer an adequate material and social environment. The good craftsman takes responsibility for and is engaged upon whole-tasks: children must similarly feel in control of whole processes. Finally the aesthetic or artistic outlook is a characteristic of life itself – not something withheld for special occasions. Aesthetic education must connect with the child's world beyond the school.

★　★　★　★　★

Aesthetic Education seeks the enhancement of sensibility through creative encounters with sensuous forms – including the sensuous forms of art. The model I have proposed to help to explain how sensibility works makes clear that to treat forms in terms of design means making appraisals that take into account such criteria as *fittingness, coherence, authenticity, uniqueness, multidimensionality and empathy.* We have said that whereas not all these factors will always carry the same weight in any given appraisal – their relevance will be contextually determined – all three levels of sensible behaviour are at least implicit in all such actions. A picnic in the country may only significantly engage our sensibility at Levels 1 and 2; however, even such an apparently mundane event may stir a deeper response in us, evoking metaphorical possibilities not strictly apposite to the more pragmatic requirements of the occasion.

Imagination never sleeps; nor does the mind's proclivity for analogy and inference. Revelations often visit and attend us when we are most absorbed in seemingly very ordinary even rather boring and routine jobs. Before proceeding to consider what all this might mean for the arts in education I want to look a little more closely at those "conditions" that Massingham suggested in his account of the old wood-turner (see Chapter 7) as being responsible for the blossoming of true craftsmanship, for I think we shall find we can use them to supply us with an account of the principal elements of the aesthetic curriculum – by which I mean all learning in the school which is directed through encounters with sensuous forms towards the enhancement of sensibility. (It goes without saying that we would recognize there were many other legitimate purposes served by the school curriculum – mathematical, linguistic, scientific for example. All I mean to say here is that the curriculum will have an aesthetic character by virtue of whatever degree of prominence might be accorded the development of sensibility within it. I should, for instance, expect the arts and crafts to have a major, even over-riding commitment in this direction, whereas for some other "practical" subjects the aesthetic might reasonably figure as less of a priority.)

What kind of pattern or order can we discern among the factors that seem most materially embodied in the bodger's working life? If we look again at the rather random list I produced earlier, I think it will become clear that they do form a pattern and may be collected under a number of related categories. There are, for instance, the old man's skills of eye and hand, his judgement, his knowledge and experience, his pride in his work and determination to live his own life in his own way: we might, for the time being, call these skills, abilities and activities his *personal resources* – he clearly had many more than I have listed here.

Then there are his contacts with the world at large. These occur in respect of the materials he needs for his work and the rewards he obtains as a consequence of marketing his products. Each of these functions is particularly subject to the external pressures of "supply" and "demand": in other words he could quickly be in trouble if he ran out of good timber, couldn't get the tools he needed, if the market for chairs suddenly dried up and he was forced either to sell cheap or to give up working altogether. In other words there are *conditional* aspects governing and determining his work over which, for all his ingenuity, stubbornness and craftsmanship, he has little or no control. Massingham sets great store by the master-man's total oversight of and involvement in every stage of the work: the "holistic" principle in practice. He saw to the buying and felling of trees, carted them back to the workshop, sawed them through, turned and assembled the parts into the finished chair. He also saw to the pricing and marketing. In the course of all this he understandably became a highly sophisticated judge of good workmanship, a connoisseur. What we have here is a particularly intimate relationship between a range of different skills or functions – perhaps we could adopt the word "*roles*" to cover the set of relationships between the man and the activity of chair manufacturer.

A further and final element would be the bodger's *way of life*: Massingham sees a very significant relationship between the beauty and efficiency of the man's work and its organic and intimate association with the cycle of the seasons and the slow alternation of night and day. Space and time are themselves qualitatively appraised, as is the actual environment, and we are asked to conclude that there flows from such intimacy, such organic principles, a way of life that somehow supports, nourishes and sustains sensibility. We only have to think of some of the working, to say nothing of living, conditions which attend the lives of young and old today, and which Samuel Rockall refused to acquiesce to in his own day, to sense the strength of the point being made. The circumstances of life and work, the way of a man's life, will be embodied in the man he is and the works or fruits by which we know him.

Here we have, so I believe, the principal features of an aesthetic curriculum. These will be the main concerns of any teacher interested in the development of the child's sensibility. At the centre of our curriculum model will be the "encounters" referred to in our stated aim – encounters which will be differentiated in terms of a range of possible skills. The bodger not only designed and formed the chairs, he performed a complex range of traditional skills, deployed connoisseurship in every aspect of his work from buying supplies to pricing the product, was his own salesman and advertising agent. In thinking of the sets of things children might be asked to do in school it might be felt that not all these rules would always apply. Howard Gardner (1973) with the arts particularly in mind singles out four skills of which the child will have to have some experience: forming, performing, audience-member and critic. I suspect we might be happy to settle for this more limited range whilst leaving the option open to incorporate such others as seem significant and relevant to the work we are particularly concerned with. The heart of the matter lies, however, in their "organic" relationship, in their inter-relatedness: that the child should readily move from one skill to another, and have opportunities to function to a high level in each of them, and that the child should take a personal interest in and be given personal responsibility for as much of the process as possible. This is a principle that is basic to all good craftsmanship: an increasing degree of self-sufficiency.

By forming I would imply the essentially "creative" acts of problem formulation, design and fashioning that we normally associate with individual or collective acts of making. Forming would entail every aspect of what we might mean by "inventing". I prefer the word forming because of its close association with our key word "form". Performing, on the other hand, means reproducing rather than producing: the performer takes on the role of mediator between a predetermined formula (or score) for action and the performed action itself. The performer is required to supply the actions already ordained and the performance is in many respects the manifestation of this particular role. However, there are performances in which the performer is not interpreting or mediating a previously ordained or "given" action but rather acting in the forming role – for example, in dramatic and musical improvization. This is an important distinction to bear in mind. The audience-member "receives" the form – either from the former or the performer. No account, either of arts or of aesthetic education would be complete without the education of appreciation: this role involves a form of active participation on the part of the receiver since no image can live except in the imagination of the one perceiving it. As for the skills of the critic, I feel Gardner is right to include them despite the obvious objections against. It might for instance be argued that the critic is somewhat parasitical upon sensibility and that his function is both uncreative and, in his use of words, discursive rather than presentational. My own feeling is that the best critics are in many respects like the best performers: they are interpreters and mediators, their function being to help an audience "see" what otherwise it might miss. They have to draw us into the potential space. And this requires very special, creative and perceptual powers that certainly involve and excite sensibility. These four functions then will provide the principal range of educational aesthetic encounters, and we shall discuss them more fully when we come on to consider the curriculum in practice.

The quality of the individual encounter will be in large measure determined by the range and quality of the child's personal resources. Here, as we have seen, there are a number of categories to be considered. There are the basic skills of sense discrimination, manipulation and co-ordination: children will be able to distinguish and remember particular differences of colour, musical tone, surface texture and so forth, and these discriminatory skills should improve with age; likewise their powers of mental-physical co-ordination and of the manipulative control of media, tools and instruments. These are all, clearly, indispensable resources for sensible encounters with form.

There is know-how and knowledge also that are equally important to aesthetic practice. As we saw with the "bodger" although in many respects he made his work his own and gave it a characteristic quality as recognizable as a personal signature, he nevertheless worked within a tradition. His craft was the embodiment of countless individual crafting experiences: there were "rules" governing the right use of tools and the right dimensions and proportions of the article to be fashioned. Not arbitrary rules either but rules that were the distillation of experience, signposts to excellence. And every craftsman's first admitted allegiance is to that congregation of past-masters whose practice made the craft what it is now. I recently heard the poet George Czertis declare that his first audience and his toughest critics were always the dead poets of the past in whose tradition he was working. Tradition is often thought of as somehow inimical to creativity and personal expression but true traditions are never that, since they are by definition those practices tried over time and found to yield valuable results: more particularly they are living entities, subject continually to change and adaptation. Where they do become an encumbrance it is simply because they have ceased to be applied as living criteria in living circumstances and, out-lasting their usefulness have become a petrified rule book which is somehow a law unto itself. None of us acts, works or speaks without owing everything to tradition and a right use and appreciation of tradition has to be another aspect of the resourcefulness of the individual craftsman. As a hedge-trimmer I lack all sense of tradition and my former neighbour, Fred Hankin, who laid and trimmed hedges all his life, used to tremble with anger and disgust at what I achieved with hook and shears. He's long since dead, but I never pass a machine-ravaged hedge these days without thinking how it would have horrified him. His hedges were as trim and as tight as a sheep's back. Given the purposes a hedge was made to serve, such as keeping cattle, sheltering crops, marking boundaries, inhibiting the erosion of soil, there has to be a right way of making one. Fred had learned how to do it and added some learning of his own, and the hedges were his masterpieces.

Equally significant to the development of aesthetic sensibility is knowledge of the way conventions are at work in all cultural practices and processes. There is, of course, a close conceptual affinity between convention and tradition in as much as both terms refer to practices hallowed or authorized by custom. However whereas the traditions of an art or a craft are usually understood as methods or practices inherent in the process of production, conventions are those devices customarily understood as signalling or signifying in a particular way. To understand the way an art form signifies, it may be absolutely essential to be conversant with its use of conventions. The more stylized, the more severely "conventional" an art form, the more obviously esoteric it is. We are all familiar with the problems posed in trying to appreciate or tune into the art of another culture that operates by conventions other than our own. The "oddness" of Japanese film versions of Shakespeare: of formal Indian dancing; of the Noh theatre; of the music of Stockhausen; of the art of the latest avant-garde painter – all are accountable for in terms of their opaqueness to conventional understanding. When we make certain allowances whilst watching a play such that an actor speaking from the front of the stage and from behind his hand, may be taken as stepping out of the drama into temporary complicity with the audience (of whom the rest of the play's characters are supposed to be quite unaware), this is a convention that we are likely to have no difficulty with once we have understood and experienced it. It is a practice established by custom and is to be understood not as breaking the play's illusory surface but as a device for enhancing the audience's sense of participation.

All the arts deploy conventional means of signalling meaning and there is a sense in which we have to admit that there can be no naive or innocent involvement in an art – all access to art is governed by a system of cultural conventions and so response to art is a factor of one's familiarity with that

system. Peter Kivy (1980) proposes the thesis that all conventional expression in music derives from what he calls the "contour" principle – that is to say
from the analogy we draw between musical shapes and the shapes of natural
expressive behaviour. Such "contours" are eventually formalized into a set of
musical conventions by means of which composers can practise upon the
sensibilities of their listeners. Kivy writes (Page 83)

> "We can think of our musical tradition as a patchwork of features of (at least) the
> following kinds: (i) Those that resemble expressive behaviour of some kind, and
> thus are heard as appropriate to the expression of something or other: for
> example, the 'weeping' figure of grief or the falling line of 'Lasciatemi morire' ...
> (ii) Those that are no longer heard as resembling expressive behaviour, but which
> are expressive by custom or convention, such as, for example, the chromatic scale
> in some of its melodic manifestations."

He continues his sketch of a theory of musical expression with the "genetic
hypothesis that all expressiveness by convention was originally expressiveness by contour" (i.e. by resemblance to natural expressive form). But that
raises the issue of conventionalized expressive communication in normal
inter-personal behaviour where such signals as smiling and head-shaking can
mean very different things in different parts of the world. It suffices,
however, for our purpose here merely to note the extreme importance of
convention as part of the signifying system of the arts everywhere and to
provide for instruction and education in the use of convention as part of an
aesthetic curriculum. It cannot possibly be all spontaneity, creativity and
expressive impulse. Even where these are plainly at a premium there will be a
fundamental debt to tradition and the deployment of convention.

Which brings us fairly naturally to a consideration of expression itself.
Whether we agree with Kivy that sensuous forms gain their expressiveness on
account of their perceived resemblance to naturally expressive forms, or
whether we prefer the idea that certain sensuous configurations (figures,
patterns, complexes) evoke feelings not by resembling them so much as by
instancing objects towards which certain feeling responses would be
appropriate – and I rather favour the latter explanation – we need some way
of accounting for the universally expressive power of sensuous "arrays".

Sensuous forms make us feel: it is not a question, as Louis Arnaud Reid
(1969) confesses, of trying to work out how feeling "gets into" sensuous
forms, and so into art. Feeling occurs naturally as our response to form. The
actual difficulty lies in keeping feeling *out* of form: and the so-called objective
sciences represent in part man's endeavour to do precisely that. To create
forms uncomplicated by any subjective, any evocative implications. Amongst
anthropoligists there has been some discussion of the idea of "expressive universals" and it is clearly a crucial idea if we are to understand
how sensuous forms can operate as signs; how we achieve the multi-

dimensionality and the integration of form with feeling that epitomizes the level of tacit operations in our three-tier model of sensibility. I was quite happy to speak of the "instructing" of children in the traditions and conventions of particular art forms though even there I suspect they pick up most of what they need (as they do for example in understanding the conventions of language and of film and television broadcasting) simply through exposure and practice. I suspect that response to the "universals" of sensuous expression is even more innate than that and is as much a function of genetic inheritance (i.e. brain programming) as of experience-based learning. And the experience bit comes so early – certainly has its beginnings before birth and is perhaps at its most intense in the early years of infant life – as to render any systematic instruction during school years more a matter of reinforcement than of induction. Which is not to say that children's sensible responses to the expressive character of sensuous forms show no development: that is manifestly not the case. Their increasingly complex and sophisticated use of materials as the means of self-expression testifies to quite the opposite.

Whether we, as teachers, can materially influence the emergence of these more complex behaviours is a difficult issue to settle. As I have already indicated my own inclination is to work very hard at providing the conditions in which sensibility is free to function in a focused way and then to plug into the child's inveterate and irresistible natural tendency towards mature sensible behaviour to inform my instructional decisions. I think I know broadly what to expect of "normal" aesthetic development so I'll be able to say whether or not it seems to be happening. I also think I am learning how to remove the blocks and to provide acceptable ("good enough") conditions of growth. I know I don't know how to release or structure the major developmental shifts of sensibility, artificially as it were – any more than I know how to force the move to "formal operations" in the behaviour of the child still functioning at an earlier or lower level. Perhaps the best that education can do is to reinforce a predetermined sequence of events – in which case the issue revolves about the questions "What reinforcement?" "When?" Where sensibility is concerned there seems good reason never to force the pace of a child's progress, and every reason to allow regression, practice and idleness. Our task as arts teachers is to provide the conditions which will encourage the individual child to function fully at a level appropriate to his or her experience and needs.

But our model reminds us that it is the function of sensibility not simply to discern – and perhaps exploit – the expressive qualities inherent in sensuous forms, but to elicit the intrinsic character or identity of such forms by, in some sense, apprehending the structural principle inherent in their design. This is as much a perceptual as a conceptual matter because we experience such apprehensions of integrity and particularity much as we apprehend the personality of a human acquaintance: we *feel* their singularity, their presence. We might be able to point to a general concept such as "wave-like" or "serial" or "spiral" to indicate the principle of design that is apparently responsible for the way a particular object is, but the thing, apprehended of and in itself, is something not just classified conceptually but felt immediately. It is experienced directly as affecting us. So, at Level 2, we concentrate on this feature of singularity or charismatic identity. Level 1, as we have seen, concerns our perception of the thing as fitting – by which we mean coherent in every possible respect. So sensibility accounts on the one hand for our capacity to discern kinds of coherence in structures of all sorts, and on the other, to discern the affective meaning inherent in all such forms. What we might call the psychological response is dependent upon the perceptual (or cognitive): we feel only in so far as we can actually perceive form (coherence).

Despite everything we have said concerning the child's natural or spontaneous development towards aesthetic maturity, there is a crucial sense in which the discerning of form depends upon knowing what counts as form, and that will be in very large measure culturally determined, be specific to the culture into which the child is born. It would be absurd to say that anyone but an "expert" would be capable of making really fine judgements about the quality of a particular chrysanthemum, mathematical computation, move in chess, "tune" of a racing car engine and so forth. We rightly speak of an "educated" ear, nose and palate – and these are not to be despised merely because in the past their education has been mostly the prerogative of a privileged minority. At a more general level any intelligent musical, literary or other artistic response will depend every bit as much upon knowing the conventions or the rules that govern each system as, for instance, the understanding of the highway *code*, the *laws* of cricket and the *order* of a church service. It has long been a debateable point how far we feel we can rely on unstructured, informal cultural encounters to induce the appropriate response, and how far a formal system of educational instruction – induction – should be involved.

All in all, so far at least, despite my reservations in some respects, there appears to be a good deal of scope for teaching in aesthetics and in the arts. We have pointed already to skills of handling and discernment, we have seen the powerful intervention of tradition and convention in determining our sensible responses. Now we see how sensibility itself, for all its natural and spontaneous growth, must be affected by experience and, it would follow, may be experientially educated, could in fact not function half as well as it might or should unless it were so educated. We are indeed a far cry from merely providing children with pictures to look at and paints to dabble about with. The demands we wish to make and must make of sensibility are far removed from, far more complex than might have sufficed in the Garden of Eden. All men born into mature, cultural systems have sensibilities to educate. The question we are trying to resolve is how best to educate the sensibilities of children born into our own culture and into our present times.

There are I think two further aspects of what we are calling the personal resources of sensible behaviour that materially affect its success. Samuel Rockall became the master-man he was because he made severe demands of himself. Every true craftsman must reach the point where the tradition is no longer outside, beyond or behind him but alive and well and living, as it were, within him. So his values are the values of a living system and his judgement the manifestation of a particularly refined (or "qualified") sensibility.

There has to be a sense in which education, like life, must affect *the qualification of sensibility*. This qualified sensibility allows for all the qualitative decisions the craftsman will make – or the child for that matter – whether encountering materials as former, performer, audience or critic. We are I suppose still talking about sensibility, even here, but of sensibility qualified through the exercise of its discriminatory powers: as making choices, judgements of value and quality. When we make our own judgements on the basis of aesthetic criteria we are demonstrating the quality of our sensibility and in this sense a man's values and his sensibility are one. A feature of this kind of judgement-making is its intrinsic quality: the judge need go no further than his own "qualified" intuitions. You develop a feeling for what is right – a kind of aesthetic conscience. We feel we know – "face to face" – no more looking through glasses darkly. No more checking in the book of quantities or looking through the specifications. No more casting a backward glance to the "old ones", or waiting to see what the boss will say. You just know. You know it's good; you know it's good enough; you know it's no good. And it matters not who gainsays you. Coming to know like that is surely the goal of every educational project: it is unmistakably the hall-mark of aesthetic knowing. It is a confidence not won or granted easily, particularly to or by children in school where the rule seems rather to be, "Do what I say", "Deliver the goods" (meaning someone else's goods) – and "Hang what *you* think or feel about it yourself". Aesthetic education can never be satisfied with such knowing, for intelligent feeling, sensibility, is the most immediate and most intimate form of knowledge available to us. It is a knowledge in which we are deeply implicated. To look for objectivity or mediation in such circumstances is like trying to test for heartfeltness on an ECG machine. If we cannot claim personal knowledge and know its truth or falsehood as something felt at the quick of our being we are hopelessly alienated, fractured, split. We can never be whole, hale or holy. Perhaps one of the most vital functions of the arts teacher is to call (or recall) the child to that quality of knowing, to qualify him in "face to face" encounters through the validity or otherwise of his own judgements.

I said there were two other aspects of the category "personal resources"; the second is "attitude". We have a sort of egg/horse-chicken/cart situation here inasmuch as the kinds of attitudes that appear to be prerequisite of aesthetic experience seem themselves to be the product of such experience. We have spent some time considering the notion of "cordiality" – and there is a sense in which aesthetic experience not only works upon us as a cordial, invigorating the heart and stimulating the vital spirit, but that we need to approach experience in precisely this spirit, or frame of mind, if we are indeed to benefit from the cordial effects of a good book, or a pleasant walk, a chance encounter with man, God or nature. It is the familiar and irritating story about things being given only to those who already have them. The only sense I can make out of it is to assume that man is naturally cordial by disposition and given a reasonable chance will approach the world with cordiality rather than, say, with either suspicion or malevolence. Which would imply that if we can establish the right conditions for our work with children – and we are beginning to see that doesn't just mean putting their work up or dimming the lights or playing pop music all the time – if we can establish the right conditions we may be surprised at the level of cordiality achieved and, in consequence, of the refinement of sensibility that then becomes possible.

Berger, writing about his field, spoke of the need to look "in a certain way". He doesn't say precisely what he means by this but it becomes clear enough that he is talking about perceiving aesthetically – sensibly. If your attitude is wrong: if you are worried, nervous, anxious; if you are sick and perhaps suffering; if you are hungry or "on the run"; if you are angry, envious or self-important; if you want to make or turn a quick penny; if you are simply tired out, or perhaps facing an emergency that must be dealt with – all these things will put cordiality to flight just as swiftly and just as tragically as Lear's anger, impatience and stupidity put Cordelia to flight. No one has a divine right to cordiality (and even Samuel Rockall must have had his bad moments). But we all know those who are disposed towards the kind of thing I mean by cordiality and we know that they are the people who see visions, who are genuinely gleeful and exuberant and who know life as abundant. Perhaps it is not too much to infer that a life that respects the conditions of cordiality might promote the experience of the same. Be that as it may there can be no sensibility without a predisposition to view the world in a certain way – essentially as sacred, or sacramental.

CHAPTER 9

A Cultural Education

If we look at the lives of young people today we find, on the one hand, a frightening lack of expressive opportunity, and on the other the spontaneous erruption of sub-cultural styles indicative of the intensity of their expressive needs. Aesthetic education has to come to terms with both these phenomena and must align itself directly with the pupil's actions as life-stylist. Arts education as cultural education means responding to the young's needs to generate individual and group identity – to make a significant mark. Whilst in no way disparaging the vocational aspect of formal education I would want to argue that there was never a greater need to equip children and young people to discover and create personal meaning in the world and to discover the values of communitas and the uses of sensibility.

★　★　★　★　★

We have looked at two features of our curriculum model. We have placed aesthetic perception at the centre and identified four basic skills, namely forming, performing, attending and mediating. We have considered the range of personal resources that would seem to be relevant to aesthetic experience and given pride of place to the operation of a "qualified sensibility". The third feature we must consider is the relation between the individual life and the real world – the world of material objects, of other people, of society in general: what we might call the environmental or cultural conditions of the aesthetic life. We know for instance that Samuel Rockall's way of life had a particular quality about it: for all the speed with which he worked and the burden or strain his work placed upon him, his life had a homogeneous, a seamless quality about it and was governed by rhythms that were rooted in natural events rather than mechanical ones. He worked no night shift one suspects but, like most country people, rose at dawn and went to bed soon after sunset; he would have set Sunday aside – and possibly most of Saturday also. There would have been no "overtime". Long hours undoubtedly. The resources he needed stood a short walk from his workshop – and customers came to him with their orders. Such spare time as he allowed himself was spent either with the family and family concerns (for example making toys and utensils for family use) or relaxing with his fellow workers, perhaps singing and drinking. Massingham's account says little about the way Rockall found entertainment or relaxation: we may be sure though that the singing, dancing and story-telling that were then the staple leisure occupations would have figured in his life as in the lives of all his own folk and of his counterparts in the mining and manufacturing communities of the new industrialized parts of the country: Wales, the Midlands, the North East.

There is an important sense in which the bodger's way of life, his values and attitudes, would have found *expression* in the quality of the work he did, in the kind of family and home he made with his wife and children, in his and the family's interaction with the community of which they were a part. He will have found in the wood he worked with and the chairs he fashioned sufficient scope to realize or actualize himself: to make and leave his mark. Making your mark is perhaps the most insistent drive you have after the means of life have been supplied – and the quality of the mark we make is an aesthetic matter. Work has for generations been one way in which a man might make and leave his mark; there are those who would argue that women on the other hand have never had the opportunities for mark-making that were traditionally open to men: i.e. occupation, unless one allows – as I think we might – the making of the home as means of self fulfilment. These days of course, and indeed for some time now, the scope for mark-making, or mark-leaving, through work has been steadily eroded. Women and men have been doing the jobs of robots for many years: the only difference now is that the robots are finally claiming that kind of work for themselves and leaving the human with nothing to do whatsoever. I have already suggested that work is one way we can feel we are changing the world, altering circumstances, answering the desires and longings we are aware of, easing the pain and frustration we feel. Even a job that we call "soul destroying" can leave you at the end of the week with the means to make up to yourself for all that boredom and waste. There is the weekend; there is the night; there is the holiday. Border country where another kind of reality awaits us.

As work becomes either less intrinsically satisfying (by offering fewer expressive opportunities) or simply less available, there is bound to be an increasing pressure to find other expressive outlets. The alternative is to deal with the expressive drive by anaesthetizing it. With unresponsive surroundings (i.e. housing constructed of plastic, concrete and polystyrene – no gardens), overcrowding, isolation and pollution as permanent features of one's daily life, the expressive problem becomes even more acute. People on the one hand are subject to pressures of all kinds (irritation, anxiety, confused feelings) which increasingly demand clarification and release in expressive activity, and on the other hand are given fewer and fewer satisfactory outlets for their expressive energy. It doesn't take much imagina-

tion to see in this situation the grounds for massive personal and social
disorder. The anaesthetic solution will attempt to reduce sensibility –
essentially so you won't feel the pain any more, the point being that
sensibility leaves us open to pain as well as pleasure, ugliness as well as
beauty. In a sense it could be deemed the greatest cruelty, not to say
absurdity, to develop and to qualify sensibility in those who can only suffer
the more intensely in consequence. Like educating women and then expect-
ing them to mind the home for the rest of their lives. Or like an
education-for-work ethic in schools when more and more children leave
qualified only for the dole queue. The anaesthetic solution can mean the
drugging or inhibition of sensibility. It can also mean suicide or suicidal
tendencies. It is anti-life.

Different lives need different forms of expressive outlets depending on the
ratio of impulse to opportunity. Given a moderate level of circumstantial
problems and an adequate range of opportunities for rendering feeling in
form (home, work and recreation) there is a good chance of a reasonably
well-adjusted life. Given an imbalance between sensate disturbance and the
means or opportunity for expressive resolution we have a rising likelihood of
reactive breakdown. It stands to reason that decisions about educational
provision have to take account of people's needs and prospects. One powerful
argument at the moment in favour of increased and more effective educational provision in the aesthetic area would seem to be what we might call the
expressive crisis arising as we have seen on the one hand from the increase in
the problematic character of daily life and on the other from the rapid erosion
of the opportunities for marking one's being hitherto afforded by occupation
or work. I hasten to say that it is not the same as to argue that we need more
arts education because there will be more leisure time and people will need
more ways of passing or killing time (i.e. more hobbies).

It is perhaps like saying that whereas people formerly found expressive
outlets and interest in work – in occupation – we may expect a swing towards
other sources of stimulus and identification. Identification is obviously very
important for our purposes since we are known to others and become aware
of ourselves through the marks we make. We can perhaps see this shift of
expressive ground and this seeking after new centres of interest most
particularly in the so-called "sub-cultural" activities of the young. Teenage
sub-culture has been the subject of a number of fascinating studies recently,
and I want briefly to draw upon two of them: Paul Willis's *Profane Culture*
(1978) and Dick Hebdige's *Subculture* (1979). Here for instance is an excerpt
from a group interview reported by Willis:

> "Harry: It (pop music) played a big part in making me the way I am now …
> John: The music's dangerous, I think, it becomes something and you start
>   to think, which doesn't suit the government, the leaders … it's
>   dangerous because it makes people look at themselves and look
>   around and see exactly how they've been suppressed …

Sue: It changes your life, it changes your outlook on life, music is a development, it's a development of life ... it changes your social habits." (Page 163)

The way music has become not simply a source of pleasure for the young but, increasingly, a medium of expression and a means towards identity is one of the most fascinating aspects of the history of "pop". The relation between the music and the life is made clear in another interview:

"Les: The bands that are producing music today are coming out of this life-style, they are only projecting what we are thinking. They are coming from this life-style, they are growing from us, and they are communicating what we already know." (Page 163)

Willis comments:

"We must recognize the hippy achievement in developing such a close and relevant relationship between music and a social group. It holds many lessons. Certainly the music must not be written off as "mad" or as the insubstantial candyfloss product of cynical commercial manipulation. Though this and the other pop music is produced under capitalism as a commodity, there is a profane power amongst minority and oppressed groups to sometimes take as their own, select and creatively develop particular artefacts to re-express their own meanings. The determining system of commercial interests, and the limited imagination of the dominant order, can be transcended at the level of living day-to-day relationships. The trivia which trap us can be turned against what lies behind them." (Page 166)

In his assessment of the appeal of rock-n-roll music to the motor-bike boys Willis notes how the emphasis upon rhythm and the suppression or break up of melody permits a close identification between feeling and form. It emphasizes timelessness, immediacy and a concrete, participatory drive that is the stamp of the boys' commitment to masculinity, aggression and sensation.

"Most crucially, this music allows the return of the body in music, and encourages the development of a culture based on movement and confidence in movement ... The eclipse of tonality and melody in the music is also the eclipse of abstraction in the bike culture." (Page 78)

Willis concludes this section of his book with an interesting assessment of the relationship between rock music and bike riding that curves back to our earlier exploration of the aesthetic as anti-pragmatic in the sense of its being beyond time and spaced-out:

"Hearing the steady strum of the motor-bike exhaust (reminiscent of the 'pulse' of their music) riding nowhere in particular ... is a steady state of being, not a purposive, time-bound action towards a functional end. In a curious way, death on the motor-bike stopped time altogether: it fixed and secured this symbolic state for ever. In sum, they were exploring a state, a space, rather than a linear logic." (Page 78)

Hebdige's book documents and assesses the whole range of youth sub-cultures since the 1939–45 war but concentrates particularly on the nature and meaning of the white punk and of the black reggae movements. Like Willis he sees these music-based groupings as serving essentially "expressive" ends. The dead-pan, alienated, " lumpen" faces and postures of the punks, with their calculated raggedness, emaciation and dissonant ugliness, serve both as an embodiment or instancing of their hopeless and dead-end lives and give the lie to such an assessment in the strength and irony of the defiant gesture that they make. They have chosen to make death the "evocative image" of life. As for the black Rastafarians, their reggae music has been both the expression of and an incitement to a sudden sense of their own worth. To be black is suddenly prized: it is also full of "dread" and a hitherto exploited, humiliated and reviled minority has found dignity and self-confidence in an act of triumphant self-assertion. If ever there was body in music it was a black body and the music was the music of black Africa. For both these groups music has given embodiment to the feelings of resentment and frustration that come of underprivilege, and their distinctive styles – of dress, move-ment, gesture, facial expression as well as of music – provide a complete inter-arts system of expressive self-revelation and self-identification. Shorn of all other visible outlets these youth cultures have made life expressive, perhaps in a way that once it was but certainly in a way we have been quite unused to and were not prepared for. It is the very opposite of high-culture in as much as we are speaking here not so much of creating an impression as of giving expression.

As I hope I have indicated these are two remarkably provocative as well as informative books. Obligatory reading for anyone interested in aesthetics or arts education. They raise some very important issues for us and perhaps expose much that is weak both in our practice and in our thinking. In the first place they serve to remind us of the centrality of the idea of the aesthetic as something lived, as a way of life. Perhaps one would say as *the* way of life in the sense that where sensibility informs choice about the style of a person's life, it has to be upon aesthetic criteria that such choices are made. In the examples we have been considering, youth "style" is expressive of youth feelings, attitudes and values: it is as if some irrepressible urge has broken up the concrete of the dominant ideology and "flowered" as those exotic forms of personal and community being. It is a demonstration that the final lesson of an aesthetic education is that life is style and style is expressive form. For style to be aesthetic it must be responsive to impulse (rather than, say, merely dictated by convention or fashion) and one of the outcomes of a successful aesthetic education will be the inculcation in the young of the possibility and then of the means to achieving a life style – a life-sign – that has integrity and will serve their expressive needs.

This could run absolutely counter to more traditional and more prevalent ideas about teaching the young what to value in the world of high culture, giving them "good taste" in the received, narrow sense. The good taste they actually need is their own; it will be indwelling in their sensibility, adapted to the expression of their own personalities and circumstances and expectations: their own pain and longing. That a knowledge of what is going on and has passed in the narrow, specialized world of the high arts, of media, design and technology might supply the means to that expression goes without saying.

It is important to remind ourselves however that expression is not to be understood as the rendering external of something that otherwise would merely remain internal, and so, private and hidden. Expression, as we have argued elsewhere (Ross, 1978) is a *creative* act. When the chosen medium (and this is, of course, essential) not only reflects back but changes the impulse in the reciprocal act of expressive projection, then expression becomes not merely the means of feeling and of releasing feeling but of achieving entirely new levels or structures of feeling. So expression becomes the means to fresh insight and fresh understanding. It opens up new possibilities by allowing the assimilation and integration of otherwise inchoate and disordered experience that has accumulated from past encounters. It is the essentially creative – and so life-enhancing – aspect of expression that makes for its importance in the daily experience of everyone and that is also why an expressive crisis, the loss of expressive opportunity, is such a personal and social disaster. Expression, as we have said so often, depends upon the act of "embodiment": style can be such an act of embodiment and therefore is one route to personal and social integration.

Given such a scenario for aesthetic education, i.e. a commitment to qualify the child as life-stylist with everything that such a programme would entail, we are bound to feel some anxiety when we consider the considerably narrower range of concerns that have constituted our focus of interest in the past. We not only have to throw out the curriculum that centres upon the substance and ideology of the High Arts – we also have to open ourselves to a concern with areas of experience that might seem to concede little or nothing to any form of art, high or low. In other words we have to take on board all those occasions of sensibility that the young are exposed to and available for – and to show how a concern with the criteria of Level 1 can hardly be prevented from opening up to the possibilities inherent at the ultimate level of tacit operations. Sign is everywhere. Making our mark is an absolute priority: if it doesn't feature among Maslow's Deficiency Needs, then it ought to. Owning – as distinct from assuming – a style is probably one of the most essential factors affecting psychic integrity and coherence. This is tantamount to saying that the Aesthetics Faculty in any school is bound to take expression in all its forms extremely seriously and would require us to have the services of all those teachers with an understanding of dress, popular music, body imagery, gesture, movement, mechanics, interior and environmental design, mental health, sport and games, gardening and all forms and aspects of culture. We are not talking about cultural *studies* (though there could well be room for such "impressive" learning within a total programme). By culture here I mean living: the generation of an identity, a body, an embodiment, a style, a mark.

Which brings us to a very awkward issue indeed: the relationship between schooling and youth culture. There have been a number of attempts to bridge the gap between the world of school and the interests of children – in particular their, dare one say, "cultural" interests. Of course there are many institutions where no one would dream of making any concessions at all and where the traditional war between teachers and kids is waged very much as it always has been subject to local variations, and with increasing commitment on both sides. The factors likely to set teachers and kids against one another, amongst others, are these: most teachers come from the literate, verbally-strong, middle classes whereas most kids come from the semi-literate, verbally weak lower classes; most teachers are white and British whereas many kids these days are neither; teachers are adult and kids are kids; teachers are outsiders whereas kids are local; teachers know it all and kids have got to learn it all; teachers are volunteers and kids conscripts; teachers are paid to work in schools, kids' work is unpaid; teachers are licensed to punish kids but not the other way around. As I say there are lots of causes of possible conflict – and all those I have referred to so far are in their way cultural.

Perhaps more particularly these days there are more obvious tensions arising out of the kind of identity-building process among young people going on outside school, and to which we have just been referring. Kids are identifying themselves increasingly as mark-makers, as signifiers – and by virtue of that very fact sense that their personal and collective definition is made *against* the values and practices, and indeed against the personnel associated with schooling. Youth cultures are deviant cultures, cultures against the adult world, against the bourgeois values embodied in schooling, against government, against the established ways, and at odds with the older generation and probably its perceptions of its class-role. Kids have not, by and large, deployed their new-found significance to any marked effect against the school system. They do not reject school examinations. Most still go to school though truancy is a good deal more marked than it was. Most kids still accept to wear uniform. Most kids still respect rather than violate and incinerate the school premises. Relatively few teachers are actually abused or subjected to violence and as far as I know there are no notices in schools, as in the tube-trains, warning about maximum penalties for assaulting staff. But alienation, cynicism, unruliness, indiscipline, non-motivation are rife. Kid culture is inveterately anti-establishment and that has got to mean anti-school. As the truth dawns upon the pupils that the schools no longer offer the only, indeed any access, to good jobs, to good money, the pressure to contain them in manageable numbers will undoubtedly increase. Kids have been traditionally long suffering when they felt on the one hand that they had little choice (i.e. no one would support their refusal), and on the other that there would be some eventual compensation for all the pain, all the boredom: an independence-giving and fun-giving pay packet. Now you can qualify for the dole without even turning up to school at all let alone slaving whilst you are there. No doubt teacher unions everywhere are being pressed by their members for guidance as the rate of stress-retirements goes up steadily every year. It will be argued that only sterner and more ingenious "policing" will meet the likely problems – certainly there will be very few who could see any point in seeking rapport or rapprochement between the two cultures.

And I am not going to suggest that the answer lies in teaching girls how to streak their hair, or to turn out bondage chains for the boys during heavy craft lessons. Any more than allowing them to play pop in the music lesson has solved the difficulties traditionally experienced by music teachers. One of the most disastrous art lessons I ever saw involved some ten bike-boys sitting at their drawing boards grouped around a motor-bike thoughtfully provided by the teacher. They could all have ridden the bike pretty well but drawing it was something they didn't find anything like so compelling. If, as we are saying, the arts, even the traditional arts, sit very uncomfortably within the secular, pragmatic, established curriculum – what about youth culture? How are we to conceive of schooling which on the one hand embodies and serves the established values of a materialist, bourgeois, adult ethic and which nonetheless accommodates not just the disruptive arts (whose role has traditionally been to question and undermine prevailing perceptions of what might be lawful and orderly) but a freely expressed, alien and enslaved youth culture? It would seem the merest common sense to keep the arts on a very tight rein and pegged somewhere near the perimeter fence, and to outlaw any expression of youth culture altogether. And this expedient is of course the norm today.

I recently came across, quite by chance, an emblem of just this policy, just this state of mind. In a Georgian Square just off London's Baker Street is a small, railed, circular garden. It looks peaceful and inviting in the sunshine. On the day I found it I could see several benches within the railings and decided it would be nice to have a sit down. I walked most of the way around the garden without gaining entry and finally found a gate. It was locked. There was a rather venerable painted notice-board attached to the gate that told me the garden was private, and that was that. Then I made out another notice equally venerable but rather more dilapidated, nailed to a post some ten yards within the railings. It warned all residents of the said square, whose privilege it was to use the garden, against a range of misconducts. All games were forbidden. Furthermore there was to be no feeding of pigeons, cats, dogs and other animals. Any leaving of the gate on the latch or, still worse, propping it ajar would be subject to the direst penalties. Children could only be admitted under the strictest conditions of surveillance: horseplay and trampling was specifically interdicted. Like all good schools this little garden was essentially a no-go area for the hoi-poloi. It was clearly reserved for persons given to such meditative acts as snoozing, genteel strolling, good-mannered conversation and silent reading. The notices said enough but the iron railings said more! The ultimate irony however did not in fact reveal itself to me immediately. There was mention of a rubbish bin and of a rubbish dump, on to which incidentally no-one was permitted to dump anything, as presumably this would unreasonably have released the gardener of his duties. I was looking about for these homely items when to my astonishment I saw, in the very heart of the garden, a tangle of freshly painted, black iron-work of distinctly recent date. I instantly took it to be a collapsed municipal lamp standard and was pondering what kind of accident might have felled it when it dawned upon me that the residents had done that thing peculiarly beloved of the collective urban mind: they'd had a whip round and bought themselves a modern Work of Art. And locked it up just to be on the safe side.

I want to suggest that we drop the idea of education for occupations in favour of the idea of education for *occupation*: i.e. for the capacity to be absorbed, possessed and seized. Such a concept is the very opposite of alienation, which is arguably the most debilitating sickness of our time. That would mean essentially shifting the ground of the educational experience from the pursuit of purely pragmatic meanings to the pursuit of cultural meaning. "Putting the body back". It would further mean that education would emphasize the quality of on-going mental, physical and emotional engagement in the here and now and largely dispense with prognosticating outcomes, products and all long-term situational pay-offs. In other words, and speaking now strictly within the context of aesthetic education, there would be no question of being guided over matters of curriculum by any notions of qualifying children for eventual admittance to the railed garden of the High Arts. Rather we should be equipping them to function as fully paid up members of the youth community and leave them to create their own adult forms later on the basis of getting themselves together now. Why should we not have a genuinely creative education – and if it is to be creative, then one focused on process, one that would not allow product to dominate and dictate outcomes in advance? There are skills, resources and knowledge that children absolutely must be given if *their* responses to life, both at school and in the wider context are to be creative: and if they aren't to be creative then what possible alternative worth giving a second thought to suggests itself?

CHAPTER 10

The System is the Enemy

Schools as currently constituted – and the DES under the present dispensation – are likely to continue to prove unsympathetic to the kinds of priorities adumbrated here. However, we must go on resisting the tendency to downgrade the concept of education to mere training and in doing so should establish our own concern as being essentially cultural – in the sense of cultivating the child's poetic spirit. Part of such a programme will inevitably involve artistic perception and creation. Children's cultural education must receive far greater recognition in the curriculum – we need a new breed of Head Teacher and a new breed of Arts Teacher to give schooling balance and a fresh direction.

★　★　★　★　★

"Are Schools the Enemy?" Harry Rée (in Ross, 1981) delivered a paper with this title at a recent Exeter University Creative Arts Annual Summer School. When the time came to prepare the manuscript for publication the title suffered an interesting metamorphosis at the typist's hands: "Our School's the Enemy!" Perhaps it was rather a pity that this interesting shift of emphasis should have been spotted at the proof-reading stage. The writer begins as he intends to continue: in a bruising and uncompromising style. Schools, he says, aren't concerned to develop feelings "because feelings cannot be competitively examined". Arts teaching as currently practised, "generally ensures rejection of and by the majority". The conditions under which the arts might flourish are absolutely frustrated by "unbendable timetables", whilst teaching has to be carried on in "snippets of time unsuitable for the pursuit of the arts". Rée lambasts his own education that has left him ... "a cultured philistine ... formed and modelled to *speak* respectfully of the arts, to be bespattered by a smattering of art history, to make an attempt to take innovation on board, and to reproduce ourselves in the next generation".

He then goes on to cite the "salutary and important influence" had upon him by Henry Morris, Chief Education Officer for Cambridgeshire from 1922–1958. Henry Morris of course was the instigator of community and continuing education in this country through his village college scheme. Morris warned of "the menace of aimless leisure amidst economic security, and of the decadence and disillusion and weariness that will arise with widespread intellectual and emotional unemployment". This is an important perception: unemployment as being without work must inevitably threaten to bring with it intellectual, emotional, imaginative and social breakdown. For all that most people's work is variously soul-destroying, mechanical and debilitating, to be actually cut loose from the work process altogether, given the education tradition has provided, is to be "culturally" shipwrecked. It is to find oneself in a spiritual, mental and affective vacuum. Morris is arguing for an education that provides people with resources to survive – preferably to develop culturally. It would appear that the charge against the schools might be well-founded. Whatever Harry Rée means when he calls himself a cultured philistine – and he hardly wishes to congratulate himself on such a categorization – the notion that schools are traditionally inept on the cultural side of education will probably receive general and ready endorsement.

I concluded the preceding chapter by saying that I should like to see "occupation" rather than "occupations" as the goal of a New Education. The New Oxford Dictionary gives the derivation of the word as "ob + capere (seize)". Of course it would be palpably absurd to suggest that schooling should renounce all its "vocational" objectives: even in the robot and computer dominated future of the manufacturing and servicing industries there will be scope for human employment. And at the level of general education, we shall still need to give children access to the basic symbol systems: words, numbers and icons – such that they will be able to handle themselves and their affairs in the new, technological world and also that specialist, "employable" skills can be developed on the basis of such a core of learning. But the "back to basics" cry we now hear so stridently issuing from some quarters of society, coupled as it customarily is with renewed pressure upon the schools to achieve better examination results and so to provide more, qualified youngsters to compete against each other for the fewer and fewer jobs available is surely an extraordinary act of shortsightedness.

It is probably no more sinister than that, and yet it might not be entirely wide of the mark to see in such revisionism the Establishment, the System, taking advantage of general panic and uncertainty to tighten its grip upon the throat of social deviance and challenge. There is after all, a barely disguised campaign being waged by Government to bring a systematically demoralized education system increasingly under the sway of the central authorities: a move towards the standardization and the nationalization of educational productivity. As we have seen the debate on the core curriculum was one obvious instance of this tendency, as is the work of the Assessment of Performance Unit and the endeavour to produce nationally agreed criteria for joint examinations at 16+. These moves all bear the stamp of an administration determined to have a much greater say over the practice of education, over decisions as to who should learn what, in controlling educational output and cost-effectiveness.

These moves have been and continue to be resisted – not merely out of a narrow professional self-interest but because they are seen to threaten experiment, initiative and flexibility of provision in education. In addition such moves are inherently anti-cultural, anti-creative, in that by increasing the externality of authority – by raising up the power and importance of assessors and adjudicators external to the pupil-teacher encounter – they serve to reduce that essential relationship to a more or less purely expedient or functional one. Marcuse (1979) has underlined the threat inherent in all these moves to establish the impregnable supremacy of central authority:

> "We are experiencing not the destruction of every whole, every unity, every meaning, but rather the rule and power of the whole, the superimposed, administered unification. Not disintegration but the reproduction and integration of that which is, is the catastrophe."

The whole complex, nervy, idiosyncratic, living system that is education in this country faces dismemberment and ingestation at the jaws of the DES. Which, I suppose, would make the DES rather than the schools the enemy.

But, of course, as Harry Rée implies, schools are – if not *the* enemy – then certainly *an* enemy. Most schools that is, as currently conceived and operated. The extent to which this indictment fits any particular institution may be judged later when we come to look more closely at the kinds of practices and circumstances likely to give rise to and support "occupation" and "cordiality", and possibly compare them with those more likely to engender "accidie" and faint-heartedness, apathy and morbidity: the culture of the true Philistine. I suppose we must be careful, in speaking of a culture-based curriculum, that we do not leave ourselves open to misunderstanding again. As we have seen already it seems impossible to adopt any of the words we need in this discussion without running the risk of being understood as meaning the precise opposite of what we actually intend! The terms "aesthetic" and "sensibility" are loaded with suggestions of an effete, privileged and moneyed way of life that by its very definition outlaws the "popular" values and principles we wish to endorse. We have had repeatedly to insist that we are talking about basic, even "primitive" forms of human behaviour, most immediately and most naturally evident in the playful behaviour of young children and absolutely the characteristic response of all life-loving people no matter what their culture, race or class. Raymond Williams (1976) upon whose illuminating discussion of these "keywords" I have relied so much prefaces his account of the words we most need with a warning such as "x" is one of the two or three most complicated words in the English language. You can be sure that if "x" were "culture" then the other two are "aesthetic" and "sensibility" (or "art" and "imagination").

From the variety of meanings of the word "culture" discerned by Williams I want to opt particularly for his reference to "the process of human development". The meaning is to be contrasted with the notion of "material development" – by which we indicate man's mastery of his environment (as a tool-maker and a user of tools), his technological progress and the institutionalization of that progress in the means of production, in the processes of rule (or regulation) and those of assertion (or war). Human development stresses the qualitative side of life and, perhaps most particularly, the practices of communication by means of which we share and negotiate values. Hebdige (1979) quotes Scholte's (1970) structural anthropologist's definition of culture as "coded exchanges of reciprocal messages" and although technological man behaves "culturally" in one interpretation of this statement it is nevertheless helpful in emphasizing the centrality of interpersonal "exchange" (i.e. communication) to the idea of culture. This particular interpretation has to be distinguished from the much narrower sense of culture as applying to the experience of the High Arts – which Williams caricatures in the mime-word "culchah". I would assert that schooling at the present time, despite all efforts to the contrary over recent years, is to be identified root and branch with the concept of man's material development, and, as such, neglects the area of human development more or less entirely. Which of course is why schools *are* the enemy.

One reason why I find the distinction between "occupation" and "occupations" so suggestive is that it helps very much to draw out the difference that I have in mind between "human" and "material" development. Occupation with its implied sense of being absorbed and possessed describes a particular *way of being*. Essentially of being locked into, at one with the object of attention. It suggests a kind of intrinsic valuing of and commitment to experience, not as instrumental to the gaining of some ulterior goal but as inherently satisfying. It stresses consciousness, responsiveness, curiosity, vitality. And, with the closely associated sense of "pre-occupation" it raises important additional notions of reverie and day-dreaming which, as we have already seen, are intimately associated with the deeper levels of direct, aesthetic experience. Education for "occupation" would be culturally based in as much as it would emphasize the development of particular human (or personal) qualities rather than the more or less complete avoidance of any such consideration in the interests of turning children into effective (or ineffective) academics.

The culture-based curriculum would not be "cultural studies". It would not be academic talk about culture – it would be a cultivating, cultivated, enculturing experience: it would cause children to engage there and then in a wide range of "encoded exchanges". Communication would be the key – acts of symbolic embodiment, enactment and transaction the purpose of which would be the development of a range of specifically human, and humanizing skills or propensities. It would be distinguished by a commitment to the immediate, concrete and direct engagement with persons and things. It would be participatory. Above all its impact would be cordial, exuberant, life-enhancing, heart-easing. Much of what is best in current arts and crafts teaching would figure predominantly in such a curriculum, but room would also be available to any other subject area prepared to offer the direct, expressive and de-mystifying approach we are talking about. Culture in the sense in which I am using it here is the expression of man's creative engagement with experience – all experience, of mind and matter, body and spirit, self and others, subject and object. What distinguishes such an education apart from its obvious commitment to conviviality is the primacy of self-engagement, of self-regulation and self-determination; the qualities of self-possession, absorption, occupation.

In his poem *Culture* W.H. Auden contrasts the insensibility of the natural world with man's inveterate and, in this instance, doom-laden sensibility.

> "Happy the hare at morning,
>   for she cannot read
> The Hunter's waking thoughts,
> Lucky the leaf
>   unable to predict the fall ...
> But what shall man do,
>   who can whistle tunes by heart,
> Knows to the bar when death shall cut
>   him short like the cry of the shearwater,
> What can he do but defend himself from
>   his knowledge?"

(Collected Shorter Poems 1930–1944, Faber & Faber, 1950, Page 62)

For Auden, the sanctuaries of culture are built upon the experience of art –

> "How comely are his places of refuge
>   and the tabernacles of his peace,
> The new books upon the morning table,
>   the lawns and the afternoon terraces!"

But it is an unequivocally High Culture he has in mind and which, typically, he both venerates and accuses – a culture purchased for the few to the cost of "the most numerous and the most poor".

> "Who with their lives have banished hence
>   the serpent and the faceless insect"

Art is man's traditional response to the fact of death, to the implacable dominion of time. Culture is the dimension of transcendence in the sense that man's "encoded messages" invariably seek to evade the trap laid by his mortal condition. Cultural artifacts are the embodiment of, to adopt the words of J.R.R. Tolkien, the "Fugitive Spirit" in man. Perhaps it seems a bit odd to ground an education upon such a principle – and yet I don't think so. For our culture is what we salvage from the entropic drift and our culture is the magic carpet we ride to the never-never lands whose promise sustains the very spirit of life itself. Which returns us neatly to our proposition that education for occupation, education that is culture-based rather than technology-based, will actually minister not simply to the earning of a "living" but to the owning of a "life". Man is cursed as well as blessed with his sensibility: our argument is that he needs training in how best to use it.

I have already presented in an earlier publication (Ross, 1975) the results of a survey of children's attitudes towards the academic curriculum. They rejected it, in favour of a curriculum that gave them more scope for personal expression and for participation in learning. They wished to be more engaged by and more immediately involved in their education. More recently there has been a wider acknowledgement among educators of the non-academic needs of children in school. This awareness has manifested itself particularly in the current vogue for what is called social and moral education – a topic that now figures high on many a Chief Education Officer's list of skills needed by the profession. It is not immediately clear why a frontal assault upon these issues should be especially effective and one suspects that most of the motivation behind this particular lobby arises from an anxiety about public dissatisfaction with innovation in education practices in general and with the actual difficulties many adults are experiencing in a society plagued by adolescent agitation and hostility. A few years ago the preferred solution to these kinds of problem lay in the establishment of the in-school counselling service and "sanctuary" (so-called), – a now widely questioned expedient. What are the likely prospects for actually affecting children's behaviour and attitudes of a study-package designed to exercise moral and social intelligence? There is a good chance I would say of much "dilemma" solving at the level of intellection and little discernible rise in levels of moral and social performance. Whereas a culture-based curriculum that embodied, because actively engaging, the child's moral responses, might be a different matter altogether. It seems endemic in all educational innovations to reduce actuality to exercise and participation to speculation – tendencies which, certainly in the sphere of human action, and of knowing as action, invariably prove self-defeating. What we actually need is not an education in or for morality or sociability but an education that is inherently cordial and convivial, i.e. moral and social.

Let us by all means cry "Back to the Basics" – but let us also be clear what we might actually be understood to mean. Not, for certain, the so-called basics of the now discredited and outmoded academic/vocational curriculum!

I would want to identify the basic purpose of education as being cultural – as for instance it still very much is in our best infant and junior schools. In such places the primacy of "occupation" as a supremely important educational experience is recognized. Children learn sociability through inter-personal encounter and exchange; their moral development is similarly nurtured. Back to Basics – for me at least – means quite simply "the return of the body" in education. It means redressing the balance of education, recognizing the claims of intuition, imagination and feeling, allowing that "encoded messages" are not confined to the medium of words and indeed have their beginnings at the pre-verbal (i.e. "semiotic") level. It means recognizing the prime important of human expression and the crucial importance of externalizing the inner world in order to give it coherence and allow feeling to inform action. Above all Back to Basics as an invocation of the aesthetic principle in education has to bespeak the being of the child, has to remind us of the personal world each child brings to school – a world where important events take place and within which the child must feel at home if his or her actions in the world of objects are to be at all reliable, effective or comprehensible.

The world "within" is literally *embodied* – housed by the body. The body is its most immediate medium and so it is hardly surprising to find that our feeling experiences are imaged and represented in corporeal terms. The body is our first expressive medium as it is the source of all personal imagery – hence of our conception of ourselves. "The return of the body" in education would not be at the expense of the mind; it would be in recognition of the body's own cognitive function: knowing at one's fingertips. A culture-based education is primarily experiential: it feeds and answers to the qualitative problems in the child's own life on the assumption that there can be no better preparation for the future than "right doing" in the present. I think we may safely assert that if we have managed to keep pace with and supplied the means of solving the increasingly complex sensate problems children encounter growing up we shall have given them the surest possible root-system for the sustaining of their own human as distinct from material development. They will have become "cultured" in a really important sense of that word.

We should now, perhaps, try to draw together some of the consequences of such a view for the curriculum as a whole and for the arts curriculum in particular. If we concede that at all levels of schooling there should be adequate provision for the child's cultural development – and I would expect there to be at least a 50:50 ratio at the most academic extreme between "human" and "material" provision, we are going to need a new breed of Head Teacher and a new breed of Arts Teacher. More than that we must expect every aspect of teacher education (initial, further and in-service training) to reflect this shift of concern both in nurturing the teachers' own human growth and in giving the teacher some real understanding of human growth in general and of the affective and aesthetic development of children in particular. I am saying that this sort of provision should be the staple of every programme of teacher training. The cry now of course is, "Let every man know his computer!" Probably no bad thing. But there is an older, more basic, more heartfelt cry than that: "Let every man know himself." Not know *about* himself as you might be said to know about the human body through studying and assimilating the information provided by those gruesome body charts one sees hanging on anatomy department walls. Knowing yourself, in the sense that I am speaking of, means participating continuously in the expressive behaviour whereby feeling achieves coherence through the mediation of form – and we have seen that this is the essence of all aesthetic understanding. By the way of Embodiment – by the return of the body.

We need a new breed of Heads who will not only, because they have been given the appropriate training, be able to understand the importance of human expressive behaviour but will know something of the conditions necessary to the development of sensibility and be able to make intelligent and imaginative response to the questions and needs of their staff. Theirs also would be the task of educating the parents – one likely to be a good deal easier in the future since the next generation of parents is going to be sympathetic to the cultural argument given their own perhaps relatively enlightened education in the arts and their first hand and bitter experience of the failure of the academic curriculum. We need new arts teachers also because, certainly at present, for all the excellent work being done for the student teacher as artist (actor, instrumentalist, literary critic) in the standard "Main" course, the so-called professional training of potential arts teachers is almost universally ineffectual. I am thinking particularly here of the total lack of concern for the kind of issues raised in this essay: the relation of principle to practice, the need for and use of a conceptual framework, the notion of aesthetic development, the problems of assessment and validation in arts education. Perhaps even more importantly the understanding of the way sensibility works and develops and the consideration of the need for "right conditions". Arts teachers at present have the sketchiest of notions about these absolutely critical ideas and hence collapse when faced with the task of giving anyone a reasonably clear and concise account of what they are doing, why and how well. And the shame lies not simply in one's not having anything to say, in being struck totally dumb by the most reasonable of enquiries (given that they are responsible to children, their parents and society in general for an apparently serious area of education). It lies in the fact that no coherent philosophy is available to inform their work and support their professional judgements – or not one that they can wholeheartedly endorse.

We might then have some hope of schools being no longer the enemy. Perhaps something would be done about the "unbending timetabling" – and the enforced teaching in "snippets" which Harry Rée so rightly condemns. In his paper already referred to Rée makes further mention of Henry Morris, this time talking about the aesthetic climate of the school as a cultural environment. Morris apparently abhorred "reproductions" – presumably preferring the school or the education office to supply originals instead. "I'd rather hang a dead cat on the wall than a reproduction", he is alleged to have announced on one occasion. (Today there would be a good chance of some child overhearing and obliging him). He is also reported as having told the Head of one of his village colleges to take the children's pictures off the walls of the entrance hall as it made the place look like a school! One suspects he really wanted it to look more like the Louvre or the Uffizi Gallery. I don't think I would. We must assume people will want to please themselves about the image they present to the world: the image of themselves and of their home for instance. The school Head and Governors may well wish to produce a sense of excellence or sense of achievement in the ceremonial area immediately accessible to the visitor from outside – and a changing exhibition of children's work (not just their art work) could well be appropriate to that end. On the other hand the collecting of expensive art objects may, I feel, be a good deal less easily defended. I personally like my work-space to have the feel of work and of me about it and I have always preferred to work in school-rooms and spaces where one was free to show work in progress, assemble various kinds of stimulus material and leave unmistakable emblems of oneself about the place. But people have different tastes in these matters and it will be very important to create spaces that tend to release expressive feeling and sensibility for all concerned – rather than their having to work very much against the grain in some hostile or inhibiting milieu.

On a recent working visit to Greece I watched an entire school staff spend two days prior to the beginning of the school year putting up posters and assembling mobiles, pinning up photographs and generally creating what commonly passes for the "stimulating" environment school children apparently need. The final effect certainly delighted all the adults present but I sensed its actual impact upon the children might have been marginal and short-lived. I wonder why the kids couldn't do the decorating for themselves, and whether a more flexible, more spontaneous approach mightn't have paid a more handsome educational dividend. The way the learning or living environment looks and feels is of the most immediate concern to the idea of the aesthetic in education. But we should note there are alternatives to the aesthetic or coherence of Messrs Neat and Tidy, and your personal decision will or should reflect your educational objectives.

My first reaction arriving late on a winter's Saturday evening in London recently was one of disgust and apprehension. There was filth apparently everywhere. On the pavement outside the underground station a drunk was openly urinating; down in the subway was a tangle of lavatory paper, presumably left over from a football match. The walls were wildly decorated with graffiti and on the steps at the end of the tunnel, two girls with green hair and death mask faces swayed together struggling for possession of a transistor radio. And nothing about the next half hour's walk in the open city streets alleviated these disturbing impressions. It was only in the train next day, reading descriptions in a Sunday newspaper of the pristine grandeur of the Moscow Metro system that I began to sense the more positive side of this apparently anarchic aesthetic. Vitality, exuberance, irreverence were the keynotes, and I began to realize that centralized values or standards, particularly when imposed by decree upon a whole people, are infinitely more destructive of sensibility than any mere local vandalism and licentiousness could possibly be. My own taste is actually for something more subdued, tamer and more private but, be that as it may, give me life rather than death! I don't want to labour the point beyond saying that environment, milieu counts in education and is due for some serious and sensitive re-thinking.

"Felix looked at her a moment, smiling. 'I hope'
he said, 'not to be thrown back on my reason'.
'It is very true,' Eugenia rejoined, 'that one's
reason is dismally flat. It's a bed with the mattress removed.' 2"

HENRY JAMES, *The Europeans*

CHAPTER 11

The Aesthetic Curriculum

Our account of sensibility offers a conceptual basis for the aesthetic curriculum. It emphasizes the fundamental experience of the sensuous and the primacy of the sense of order. We next consider the implications of qualitative discrimination, and of cherishing as a form of "disinterested interest" operative across the whole curriculum. Finally the aesthetic curriculum gives access to the experience of art, of forming, performing, attending and mediating in the arts. Every school should have its own Aesthetic Education Faculty or Department responsible for co-ordinating provision in this area.

★   ★   ★   ★   ★

If we consider now a school's more specific, more direct response to the claims of the aesthetic we shall want to recognize, in the first place, that there is a real sense in which the aesthetic may be said to permeate every aspect of school life, in as much as all subjects and all occasions allow scope for the exercise of sensibility. In our three-tier model we saw that at Level 1, that is at the most universal level, the principal aesthetic criterion was coherence. Which means that sensibility is first concerned to create order, to find pattern in perception. At the second level we find authenticity coupled with particularity (or uniqueness). We have said that authenticity is our sense that we may "believe" our eyes, and ears and hands etc. The need to believe at this level is of course closely tied to the survival instinct itself: it goes without saying that every deception leaves us vulnerable – unless it is (as in some forms of art and of entertainment) a deception we are prepared to allow or indulge. We have already seen that these predispositions in favour of coherence or order and of truthfulness and particularly permit us to make qualitative sense of and fully encounter all sensuous and imaginative experiences. I don't think I have to argue that sensibility defined in these terms is to be found at work throughout the range of subjects in the curriculum. Furthermore when we say there is an aesthetic of science, maths, history, geography and language for instance, we mean that each of these disciplines is itself a significant form and will give rise to its own criteria of quality (fittingness), its own distinctive permutations of the principles of "order" and "variety". One senses that at the heart of these basic aesthetic criteria lie very practical imperatives: efficiency and adaptability are of the utmost importance to the continued survival of even very primitive life forms. The most rudimentary programmes of the brain, as J.Z. Young (1980) has said are in the final analysis aesthetic. It simply remains for us to point this out to those of our colleagues who might not otherwise have thought either of themselves as having a responsibility for children's general aesthetic development or of their own subjects as fundamentally "aesthetic".

I don't want to suggest that all acts of forming, performing, attending and mediating at Levels 1 and 2 are confined to these somewhat restricted criteria. There is, as I have already said, always scope in any sensible act for the experience to deepen to Level 3 – for everyday events conceived and undertaken in purely pragmatic circumstances to achieve the level of the tacit or metaphorical. But the simple point here is that such an extension is not in itself necessary for an experience to qualify as aesthetic.

As we have seen, at Level 2 there is a clear commitment to some degree of detachment by which I simply mean that the aesthetic experience reflects some element of framing, of removing the object of attention from the environment flux, or decontextualization. When we say for instance that at Level 2 we are interested in the thing for itself, in its own right, we are to some extent (though not entirely) prepared to consider it abstracted from the world of cause and effect, of pragmatic logic. Our "general" criteria of aesthetic value are "coherence", "uniqueness", "fit" and "authenticity". We dwell upon whatever makes the thing "whole", particular, good of its kind and true.

All schemes and models are subject to over-simplification or tend to trivialize complex issues but I hope, nonetheless, that there may be some use to be made of this notion of the levels of sensibility. It has certainly allowed me to make some sense of the complex relationship between the notion of the aesthetic and the more specialized concept of art for instance. With Level 3 it seems to me the specialized business of "poetic" education begins. I am not saying that Levels 1 and 2 do not involve specialist responses: that would be absurd since we have already argued the need for educated discrimination and medium control. However, whereas we might reasonably insist that all teachers were teachers of the aesthetic in terms of Levels 1 and 2 criteria, it would not be reasonable to make the same claim with respect to Level 3. If Level 1 commits us to the perception of structural coherence and Level 2 to a concern for the "spirit" of particular forms, Level 3 with its special interest in the imaginative and expressive dimensions of perception proposes what I want to call "the poetic *sign*". First Structure, then Spirit, and then Sign. By sign here I mean the capacity for form to beguile perception: to invite and evoke the savouring of design for its transcendent or tacit meanings. What we have called "sign" is the property of all phenomena in the world. A pile of drainpipes, a lorry-load of timber, the movement of a tree's shadow on a garden wall. The simplest implements laid upon a bare table in preparation for a meal evoke a particular feeling. The rush of heavy seas breaking upon a rocky shore, the curve of "cats eyes" on a hill at night, smoke spiralling upward from a bonfire, the sudden cry of peacocks in a wood at dusk. Forms become signs when we allow ourselves to be beguiled by feeling. As I say all objects framed become "texts" and can resonate in this way – but there are special fields of human activity which would exploit "signing" as of central concern: they are those activities to which we give the special name "art".

The aesthetic pleasure or satisfaction of Level 2 is associated with our sense of things being inherently good in themselves. Above all it is the perception of the thing as unique: not merely of data having coherence but of a "form" worth savouring and cherishing, and, where man-made forms are concerned, having quality, or craftsmanship. It follows therefore that, for me at least, an identifiable and specialized Aesthetics Policy concerns all those disciplines with a commitment to craftsmanship, in the sense in which I have used the word. It boils down, very crudely, to delight sought and taken in getting things right, in being in good shape, in good form of every kind. An emphasis that is, I think distinguishable – if not "quite distinct" – from the general capacity to perceive coherence (Level 1) and the more esoteric interest in fictional forms (signs) that I believe to be the key to the poetic function of art (Level 3). Physical culture, environmental design, fashion, food are all obvious but far from being the only candidates for inclusion at this point – wherever craftsmanship and design give due weight to the demands and delights of right making there is an aesthetic commitment and an aesthetic obligation. It is recognized at the outset that pupils' concerns will range from the purely practical to the purely decorative. To admit an aesthetic obligation at Level 2 simply means acknowledging a paramount interest in, indeed passion for quality in all "crafts" no matter what their function.

So we come to the purely metaphorical or imaginative aspect of the aesthetic: I am going to talk about the arts, obviously – but not just the arts. All works of art, all artifacts and all objects may signify poetically: perhaps I should rather say, by transfiguration. Here, most particularly, we find the imaginative power of metaphor at work: objective phenomena assume expressive significance and affect us as significant "presence". At this level of sensibility, of conscious feeling, phenomena become numinous – which is what I meant earlier when referring to the essential function of art as visionary. The numinous is a special dimension of the object – literally it means to bow before in reverence, to treat as sacred, with the spirit in-dwelling. Which returns us to David Jones and his interesting reading of "sacramental" as "sign" – as signification. The sign gains signification or meaning: it does so by means of a transformation – I think I actually prefer the word transfiguration. If we can simply keep out the narrower and more common implications of the word "sacrament" we may yet be able to see how the signs of art affect us by being present to us, incarnate, incorporate, made flesh – as "encoded exchange" directed precisely at the imagination. It is to the imagination that art addresses itself; it is in the imagination that artifacts achieve the dimension, the resonance of sign, of sacred revelation, of the numen. Imagination, in this interpretation, becomes the ground of all artistic significance; in this case, since the signs are embodiments, since the sign is BODY, the significance is emotional, affective, expressive. Body is the medium of expressive knowing: imagination reads body as signifying heart: i.e. cordiality. In and through body (human and material) feeling achieves significance: body signals are decoded by the imagination which posits the substance of our "reciprocal exchanges". Level 3 therefore is the level of the expressive; it is the level of the "body's" transfiguration into sign, sacrament, numen, poem.

It is the transfigurational aspect of artistic appraisal that gives us the notion of art as fiction – with the implication that this act of bodily transfiguration posits another world, a "made" world, a fiction. Only imagination can constitute and negotiate a fictitious world – a world that stands at the opposite pole from the pragmatic world of everyday. At Level 3 sensibility is not merely disinterested – it is free, it is tacit (silent, still, beyond). At Level 3 sensibility enters the border zone, the boundary, the potential space – a possibility implicit in the earlier phases but consummated only here. What we have now therefore is our model of sensibility elaborated thus:

Level 1:   Attached or Pragmatic Attention:
            coherence as structure

Level 2:   Disinterested Attention:
            spirit in form (quality)

Level 3:   Tacit Attention:
            body as sign (numen)

Joining the Aesthetics Faculty by virtue of their commitment to and expertise in poetic sign, in the numinous, will be teachers of English, art, dance, drama, music, film and media. Level 3 embraces, of course, not simply the making and appreciation of art but ritual and myth on the one hand and on the other semiotics and the manifestations and emblems of culture as "style", both sacred and profane. I mean that clothing for instance might be considered from a purely functional point of view and, hence, subject to sensible judgements at Levels 1 and 2; might be regarded as satisfying in their own right – some such notion as "fashion" might focus study at this second level; whereas clothing as personal image – e.g. the style of the reggae blacks or punk whites documented and analysed by Dick Hebdige and referred to earlier – would clearly fit into Level 3, i.e. would be part of a syllabus concerned with "body" as sign. Now we can begin to get some idea of the subject areas likely to make an important contribution to and achieve recognition in terms of the Aesthetic in Education.

Level 1:   All Subjects

Level 2:   All subjects but especially The Crafts, Design Technology, PE, Home Economics

Level 3:   The Creative Arts, Communications and Media Studies (including Literature etc.)

The arts would be the "key" to this whole area and one might see the structure of responsibility and association in some such terms as follows:

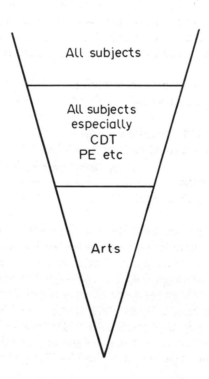

I hope this account makes clear what I mean by the aesthetic component of the curriculum. Drawing these various themes together we arrive at a matrix of *sensile action* in terms of criteria and skills. A programme of action for an aesthetic curriculum would be constituted by providing for sensible encounters in each of the four roles and as appropriate in terms of the three sets of criteria that we have established. Each subject or grouping within the Aesthetic Faculty – and all other subjects in as far as they recognized the aesthetic dimension of their work – would decide where the critical emphasis

Categories	Criteria	Modes			
		Forming	Performing	Attending	Mediating
1. Perception	Coherence				
2. Knowledge of Technique and Convention	Fittingness				
3. Attitude	Authenticity				
4. Discrimination	Particularity				
5. Imagination	Multi-dimensionality				
6. Expression	Empathy				

would lie at the stage of aesthetic development (see Chapter 13) and in relation to any given sensible occasion or encounter.

At the pre-aesthetic level we are concerned with perception alone. The aesthetic response includes, additionally, the aesthetic attitude, sensibility, knowledge of technique and convention, and creativity. All these elements when subject to imaginative transformation give us the realm of artistic communication. On the basis of this analysis it should be possible to create a comprehensive and balanced curriculum programme in this field. It would be the responsibility of the co-ordinator of the Aesthetic Education Faculty to see that provision was fully representative of the disciplines involved and that the total programme was both comprehensible and coherent. I cannot but see the argument for the "collectivization" of curriculum effort and resources within this field as irresistible. Rather the reverse: I would be very suspicious of, for example, any specialist area among the creative arts that wished to continue to go it alone, that saw no future in a collective approach such as this essay envisages. I am not sure that, in the past, the case for close collaboration and federation across the range of aesthetic subjects has necessarily been adequately argued. Still less the relation of say CDT and PE to the practices of art, drama and music teachers. This essay will have failed if it is felt that the case for coherent "togetherness" is still unclear. If, on the other hand, as I very much hope, the good sense of a shared, a united front, can now be accepted, we should perhaps give a moment or so to consider something of what such a union might mean, at the same time pointing up some of the things that would *not* of necessity follow upon the decision to make common cause.

At the very least we might expect every school to have a unified and comprehensive policy towards the aesthetic in education and that that policy would be clearly stated, available to all concerned and generally understood. Schools should appoint someone with special responsibility for this area of education and give that person the authority to co-ordinate the school's efforts at all levels – from decisions about provision for the special cases through to the consideration of the aesthetic aspects of the school as a social and working environment. The next stage would be to identify those other teachers – and subjects – which would properly fit the school's account of aesthetic education. Few nursery or primary schools at the moment have experienced and knowledgeable arts specialists but all will have teachers with some expertise in these areas. It will be important that they get together regularly for discussion about general matters of policy and curricular provision. The same would apply to the secondary and higher phases of education: there should be collective policy-making and a joint approach to all matters relating to the curriculum. My hope would be for the emergence of a distinctive style – a characteristic approach to aesthetic education – which would help lend coherence to the child's experience of the different elements within the whole.

These would be the most obvious, and, indeed, the minimum outcomes of the decision to get together. It must be made clear that there is no talk here of "integration" in the sense either of all the separate subjects being merged into one new and amorphous creature which no one would recognize, and where vital specialist qualifications would be disparaged, or of all the teachers indicated being expected to teach together, share classes or in any other way relinquish personal autonomy and privacy. It would, theoretically at least, be possible for the Aesthetic Group to limit collaboration to the agreeing of a common policy and the regular monitoring of the working of the operation – with the separateness of the individual disciplines unaffected in any other way. However that seems a position of caution bordering on the neurotic and it would in practice be more than likely that at least some of the teachers concerned would see the value of some measure of collaboration, class sharing, collective teaching and so forth.

Many schools of course have very considerable experience of these forms of co-operation among teachers, not least in respect of out-of-school activities. And teachers who have joined forces with colleagues almost invariably speak of the enhanced sense of purpose and confidence that such initiatives can bring. All that is necessary for such developments to work is that (i) the people concerned should be clear about precisely why (i.e. the *educational* reasons) they are working together and must be, if not actually enthusiastic about the idea, at least willing to be very positive, and (ii) they should be able to get along with each other sufficiently well to allow for the inevitable strains, problems and demands to be faced and overcome, (iii) there should be regular on-going joint evaluation of the undertaking and very careful final appraisal. It is often said to me that the only successful grouping of teachers has to be spontaneous and that only good friends can make a success of it. Whilst allowing that there has to be positive goodwill and a readiness to give not just good service but good companionship to others in the group, I don't feel that the notion of an "arrangement" is basically flawed. As with the "good-enough" mother the "good-enough" colleague must be able to offer at least something of himself or herself to the enterprise: I suppose the word we would want would be Illych's word "conviviality". I have personally been involved in a great many convivial enterprises that have been thoroughly successful without demanding any more by way of actual friendship between the participating individuals than either they were prepared to offer or was absolutely necessary to the project. More important than close, personal relationships is focused commitment, a strong sense of the matter in hand and of the essential part played in the enterprise as a whole by each member of the team.

Once identified the Aesthetic Group has a range of important decisions to make – so that the declared aims and scope of the group's work can be translated into a way of working, a programme. It seems to me that these decisions would have to cover at least the following topics (I have not attempted to list them in any order of importance).

1. Aesthetic Development. How does the Group – how do individuals within the Group – conceive of a child's progress or development in the aesthetic area? More particularly what changes in sensibility are discernible/desirable as children move through the school? What counts as mature aesthetic perception/judgement and how might the child's prospect of achieving maturity be best promoted?

2. Assessment. If we admit a concern with aesthetic development how do we monitor progress? What are the signals of significant development and what reliable procedure or observing and validating such development does the Group wish to adopt? What about assessment by pupils?

How often should in-school assessment take place? If "criterion referenced" assessment is adopted what criteria of attainment will be used?

3. Examination. It might be felt important to keep in-school assessment and external examination separate. There are strong arguments both for and against examinations in the arts and the school will need to decide how best to resolve the controversy to the advantage of its own students.

4. Records and Reports. What form of recording will best suit the school's purpose? What alternatives are available – for example what advantage might there be in using pupil self-report inventories? To whom should reports on aesthetic development be made, and how often?

5. Curriculum Content/Syllabus. How to conceive of "development" (see 1. above)? What kinds of experience are best suited to particular age groups and how might some experiences be seen as preparation for others? Do we want to use a ladder or a spiral or some other model of development? What sense can be made of the notion of "readiness" in the aesthetic area? Do we accept the special problems of representation usually associated with adolescence – and if so how might they best be dealt with? What experiences in the aesthetic area would be regarded as central or core, and what optional or elective? What balance does the Group wish to strike between, say, basic skills and contextual knowledge or between CDT and drama? And what about the principles of "sampling" or "cycling" or "circuiting"?

6. Inter-Departmental Structures. Would we group the arts together and the technical subjects together as sub-groups within the Faculty? It might be that within the school organization as a whole some subjects – English for example – might have a cross-faculty role (i.e. belong within the Aesthetics Group and the Languages Group). What arrangements should be made for shared working, for sharing of results, for "lead" lessons, specialist work and so forth?

7. Timetabling. Critical questions here about "blocking" and about out-of-school work. Harry Rée's "snippets" have to be dealt with – and some sensitivity shown towards colleagues on the one hand who need time allowed for setting out and clearing away, and on the other for those who prefer to work over a shorter span and more frequently. Where possible the Group wants to have total say over the detailed planning once time has been allowed by the whole-curriculum planners.

8. Budget and Resources. How to make an equitable distribution of what is allowed centrally, given the expensive character of some subjects, e.g. music. The whole question of a High Technology versus a Low

Technology approach to Aesthetic Education will have considerable financial consequences. The group will have to decide how it feels about efforts at supplementing its income.

This book does not set out to provide the answers to all these questions – such an undertaking would be quite beyond its scope even if it were actually possible. It does however attempt to establish the relevance of such questioning and to provide a conceptual basis upon which (or in terms of which) answers might be sought. However, it has to be admitted that in the present state of knowledge in the field many of these critical issues admit of only the most tentative answers. I would hope that this essay might encourage further research and investigation of those areas most strikingly underworked. Some issues identified here will however be considered in the next chapter when we think particularly about the implications of what I have been saying for education through the arts.

CHAPTER 12

Ways of Working

Kandinsky's tri-partite account of creative activity in art is explored for its applicability to arts education: impressions, improvisations and compositions. My own preference for the improvisatory mode as most compatible with the working situations commonly experienced in education is described at some length. Arts activities as "whole-tasks".

★　★　★　★　★

"Only the educator ... who knows that he offers services that should not be necessary has the humility to be courageous" (Ivan Illich: Art Education, Process and Product, Journal of Art and Design Education, Vol. 1, No 2, 1982)

This chapter is concerned with ways of working; more specifically with my own ways of working in the creative arts. And once again I shall use a quotation as my point of departure. It is taken from a letter written by the English painter Stanley Spencer. He dated it "Lent, 1917". Serving at the time in the British Army in Salonika, his imagination carries him away from the war and back to peacetime scenes of his life at home in Cookham on the banks of the Thames:

> "I walk down to the bottom of the street and call a friend, we all go down to Odney Weir for a bathe and a swim. My friend has an Airedale terrier, a fine dog with magnificent head neck and shoulders. He jumps, leaps and bounds about in the dewy grass. I feel fresh awake and alive; this is the time for visitations. We swim and and look at the bank over the rushes ... I swim right in the pathway of sunlight, I go home to breakfast thinking of the beautiful wholeness of the day. During the morning I am visited and walk about being in that visitation. How at this time everything seems more definite and to put on a new meaning and freshness you never noticed before. In the afternoon I set my work out and I begin the picture, I leave off at dusk feeling delighted with the spiritual labour I have done."

This statement has become a kind of touchstone for me. It embodies so much of what I have come to feel the aesthetic to be about. It links life and art in the sensibility of the artist. Spencer's feeling "fresh awake and alive" is surely an instance of cordiality, of life lived aesthetically, of the élan vital. And, as he says, such moments are the times "for visitations". Times when the purely bodily becomes the site of a numinous occasion. He begins his own expressive work under circumstances of intense, even if (as Wordsworth might say) "recollected" feeling. "Tranquillity" is also there in Spencer's perception of the day's "beautiful wholeness". And for all the sense of possession and ravishment implied in the description, the "real" world is not lost sight of. In fact it becomes "more definite" and puts on a "new meaning". I say it has become a touchstone for me because it contains so much of what I want my own practical sessions to achieve – most notably I suppose that sacred sense of timelessness and of being-possessed.

All that I said earlier about the numinous dimension of perception and of objective experience is dramatically realized in this piece, and every line breathes the spirit of freedom and hope, of openness and exuberance that are the hallmarks of aesthetic being. It begins with the body and passes in ravishment and ecstasy to labour. Spencer's actual process of making was curiously deliberate – as a reading of his notebooks will disclose. The "squaring-up" was all careful calculation: he seems to have been granted a vision very much in terms of the natural-world transfigured and then to have been left with the labour of composition – a labour not without its own rewards as the above passage indicates.

The Bauhaus painter Wassily Kandinsky (1977) has described his own sources of inspiration and creative rewards in a tri-partite scheme which has two psychological axes: conscious/unconscious level and external/internal stimulus. He supplies the following account of three different approaches to painting:

(1)   A direct impression of outward nature, expressed in purely artistic form. This I call 'Impression'.

(2)   A largely unconscious, spontaneous expression of inner character, the non-material nature. This I call 'Improvisation'.

(3)   An expression of a slowly formed inner feeling which comes to utterance only after long maturing. This I call 'composition'. In this, reason, consciousness, purpose, play an overwhelming part. But of the calculation nothing appears, only the feeling.

Alfred Harris (in Ross, 1982) makes the point that there is no single answer to the question "How do artists create?" – his purpose being to discourage art teachers from assuming a dogmatic position over creativity and to propose that one of the aims of arts education should be to show how multifarious are the ways of artists and the lessons of art. It would certainly seem, given the Kandinsky account, that it is possible to approach creative work with a range, if not exactly a very wide range, of motives. In fact Kandinsky implies, a little later in this particular piece of writing, that his own preferred practice is improvisatory, that is to say the largely unconscious and spontaneous treatment of what he calls "inner character", "non-material nature". I take him to be simply contrasting this approach with the two most likely alternatives: taking or making impressions of "outward nature" as a means to "purely artistic form", and the more calculated treatment of inner feeling which he calls "composition". I don't know whether it is fair to do so but I conclude from this passage that Kandinsky actually derived most of his inspiration from the act of making, from working directly in the medium. This would surely be true of improvisation where forming was largely controlled and ordained by unconscious forces interacting with perceived displacement of the medium.

I want very much to agree with Harris in stressing the alternatives available to motivate creative expression: at the same time I feel I have no reason to revise the process model I have elaborated elsewhere (Ross, 1978) which suggests that creative composition begins with the setting of the problem and proceeds by a narrowing or focusing process of approximations towards a formulation. This concept holds good it seems to me for all genuinely creative forming irrespective of the "source" of its inspiration and the practice adopted.

It so happens that I find the approach Kandinsky calls "improvisation" my own preferred way of working in education. I think this may be partly the consequence of having to work relatively swiftly and of working with large groups for only a limited period of time. I am more and more impressed by the efficacy of spontaneous – as distinct from programmed or pre-designed – aesthetic outcomes. I prefer wherever possible to keep my own suggestions when working with a group as to the theme, topic or subject matter to an absolute minimum and to rely on the dual act of engaging the medium with the senses focused to arouse the maker's imagination, that is to say to stir the imagination to scan and seek out the sensuous form inherent in what the senses perceive, and to arouse a feeling seeking form. It is extremely unusual, I find, for a simple "doodling" exercise not to arouse feeling and not to suggest imaginative possibilities, sooner rather than later. One simply has to find ways of engaging intelligently with the medium and, in suitable circumstances (i.e. the right "conditions") imagination will begin to exert its formative influence and we sense feeling seeking its "external destiny" in form.

This approach has several advantages over more deliberate "problem setting" in the arts. In the first place it allows work to begin quietly and not under the immediate influence of agitated emotion more likely to issue in a reactive than in a reflexive response. Secondly it gives the greatest possible scope to the individual maker to bring his or her own faculties into play in response to the medium – and only to the medium. This is what I am really interested in: the intimate relationship between subject and medium out of which meaning as form is achieved. The more I the teacher move into the focus of attention at this beginning stage with suggested subject matter for instance (i.e. directing the student towards "inner" or "outward" material) the less spontaneous and so the less imaginative the response is likely to be. I am not saying that I never make any direct appeal to the imagination, never suggest a starting point – simply that I find more often than not that the desired, the wished for image will emerge *spontaneously* in the action between the maker (or makers) and the medium, if the maker is free to follow his or her own intuitions. One obvious corollary of this position is that medium control becomes an extremely important element in the calculation. If you present the student with a medium – and this could of course include an instrument or tool – which he or she has great difficulty in handling and controlling there will simply be no possibility of setting imagination going that way.

The relation of maker to medium has to be one of minimal effort – I don't say of no effort at all – such that attention may of its own accord wander and the potential space open up to allow the integrating work of imagination to take place. The immediate psychic condition we are looking for is a kind of detachment, distractedness – reverie, a day-dreaming in which imagination dominates the making process and form becomes imbued with affective meaning, becomes what we have called sign or figure. Doodling with the medium – with any medium – is one sure-fire route to reverie and without reverie, nothing. Most of my own creative sessions are built upon this kind of experience and I have to be on my guard against establishing a quite different quality of attention. One, for example, that becomes too "attached" to the purely mechanical or technical problems of control, or (much worse) to speculating about what in my terms would count as a "successful" outcome of the activity. I get them day-dreaming by engaging open-mindedly (absent-mindedly) with a medium.

My task is then to check that the progress from formless functioning to forming is relatively uninterruped. By which I mean I try to "read" both the tendency of the material towards formal coherence and particularity, and the on-going quality of the student's engagement, two sets of signals that tell me what's going on. Depending upon my sensitivity at any given time and my experience of the particular student's way of working I will be able to judge when to intevene in the situation and what kind of intervention to make. I want to activate imagination. I want to facilitate expressive representation. I want to keep the student "open". I sense that this can be achieved in conditions conducive to day-dreaming. I am scrupulously careful about breaking into the dream but recognize that serious blocks or problems (for instance over medium availability or medium control, or arising from more personally inhibiting factors) always threaten the dream and in helping the student negotiate such occasions I can help protect and sustain it. The dream is the essential milieu of the poetic process.

I have recently had a great deal of satisfaction from improvisation in both music and drama. Student numbers are, I sense, somewhat critical where this kind of work is concerned and it may be that one of the greatest difficulties that arts teachers face is coping, not simply with unbending timetables but with large numbers of students at one time. I believe the expressive process in education has no meaning unless it engages each individual directly and intimately. Visual art classes allow a good deal of undisturbed collective working to individual students even if the numbers involved make individual teaching rather difficult. In dance, music and drama the simplest answer to the problem of large group management is for the teacher to take firm control over the form-making and for the class to become performers or interpreters of the teacher's ideas. I feel that this familiar device runs counter to individual expressive development and that we must either be allowed a much more acceptable pupil/teacher ratio (perhaps to be achieved by imaginative arrangements within the scope allowed to the Faculty as a whole) or train our students to work in small groups and to help each other more. I am aware that for music there are special difficulties in the over-crowding of sound-space – and of course physical space is at a premium for both dance and drama. Be that as it may we have to find the solutions we need – and the first thing is to be quite clear in our own minds why individual and small group work is so essential to us.

The plain fact of the matter of course is that in our work what counts is the particularity of the individual response. We are not demonstrating skills which we expect everyone to learn and then to perform to an agreed level of competence such that each child's performance is as near indistinguishable from the next child's as possible. Quite the reverse in fact. Individual problems, individual responses, individual style is everything with us. Even in the strongly social circumstances of the performing arts there has to be scope for and an emphasis upon individual impulse and individual from. As I say my own experience suggests that teachers of these subjects find it extremely difficult to give their work this sort of direction – so we need lots of experimentation and the sharing of solutions.

In drama I have been especially pleased with the results of two particular experiments. The first consists in requiring a class to work in groups of no more than three – and the designating of the members of each team as director, first actor (protagonist) and second actor. Any one of these individuals can be responsible for the form making – each would work in a different way and from a different perspective. The "director" might on occasions be better designated "observer" since either of the actors could "direct" just as easily. A dramatic doodle is initiated – i.e. one or both of the actors move into the empty space and the possibility of dramatic action arises inconsequentially, accidentally. Bodies move in space, meet, separate, are still, confront each other, exchange glances, words, body contact, gesture etc.

It can be the same with a small group musical improvisation: instrumentalists activate the medium by generating sound and then playing with patterns
and possible musical ideas. This notion of "idea" is important because it
quite properly suggests that the musician will know *what counts as an idea in
music*. In other words we never come to any improvisation totally naive: our
sense of what "counts" – as music or dance or drama – will derive from our
experience of these cultural forms and of the system of conventions that
governs them. Which is of course not to say that children necessarily need
formal training in musical or dramatic convention before they can improvise;
though some such training may have a use. There could be no improvised
musical "thinking" without the musical "concepts" that make such thinking
possible. There is an important sense in which apprehending a medium
means grasping the system by which meaning is achieved: becoming
"articulate". And, of course, children pick up the concepts or conventions of
their native music and drama directly, through their ears and eyes – from
their singing parents, the radio, the TV and so forth. It is the same with
dance, though we might be tempted to feel that certain bodily expressions or
gestures are universal expressive forms (see Kivy's "contour" theory) and
that all children are supplied with these expressive resources from birth. Be
that as it may, improvisation calls for expressive responses that may be
constituted as idea – and the purpose of all improvisation is to produce
"ideas" that permit of expressive exploration and development and that
answer to the immediate needs and desires of the participants.

The essential ingredient of an improvisation is spontaneous imagination –
and as Kandinsky implies this will depend a good deal upon the individual's
willingness to release unconscious impulses. Keith Johnstone
(1981) has very clearly demonstrated the threat that many people experience
in improvised activities and every teacher will want to be well prepared to
meet and cope with the dual effects of inhibition and exposure. As a teacher
you may decide to offer a minimal structure – a rhythmical pattern, a
sequence of musical intervals, two lines of speech, a simple "situation" – but
you may succeed equally well as often as not if you simply rely upon the
children to supply their own base line. More significant will be the range and
scope of the child's work and your helping the child to progress, to stretch, to
reach for more complex problems.

The small-group approach to dramatic and musical improvisation that I
have been describing allows scope for individual forming in the first place. In
practice what happens more often than not is that the individual happily
allows scope to the other people in the group and the piece becomes a
genuinely group activity. As the teacher responsible all I have to be sure of
is that the emerging artistic idea is relevant to all three participants in the
drama (if it is to be a joint creation). The other improvisatory device I am
now experimenting with gives me a more prominent function and comes

closer to a method used by many drama teachers, that is to say of participating in a class drama by assuming a role. However, acting a role in the drama is only one possibility open to me – and not the most obvious or the most typical. I mostly opt for watching and questioning the image maker, that is to say, the student chosen to initiate this particular drama from the inside (an "inside" job).

Ross:	Do you see this orchard? (indicating the open space)
Student:	Yes (cottoning on that this is a "Let's pretend" exercise)
Ross:	What sort of day is it?
Student:	Sunny.
Ross:	Is the grass wet?
Student:	No it's dry. The orchard is on a sloping hillside.
Ross:	Ah! So you can see a long way.
Student:	Yes. There's a river in the valley and a farmhouse. More hills and woods beyond.
Ross:	Take a walk in this orchard. (The student slowly wanders off and starts staring above her head and smiling.) What are you seeing?
Student:	The blossom. The trees are full of blossom – it's very beautiful. (She continues to wander about happily, taking in the place.)
Ross:	Are you alone?
Student:	Yes. Oh hang on – someone has just entered by the gate (she motions over her right shoulder).
Ross:	Man or woman?
Student:	A woman. (I return to the rest of the group – 10 in all – and ask if someone will be the newcomer. A volunteer moves across to the spot indicated and enters. She walks across the orchard in front of the original actress and stands gazing into the distance.)
Ross:	Is that right? Would she just ignore you?
Student:	Yes. She doesn't want to talk to me. She's very depressed about something.
Ross:	Do you leave her alone?
Student:	No. I go and speak to her.
Ross:	OK. Do so. What do you say to her?
Student:	I say, "Isn't the blossom beautiful. I've never seen the orchard look so lovely." Student[2] looks at her but without interest.
Ross:	What does she say to you?
Student:	She says, "The doctor still hasn't come".
Ross:	OK. (To Student[2]) Please say that.
Student[2]:	The doctor still hasn't come.
Ross:	(to Student) What now?
Student:	I put my arm in hers and we walk. (They do so, halting in another part of the orchard and separating. Student[2] makes a slight movement.)
Ross:	(to Student[2]) Do you want to sit down?
Student[2]:	Yes. (She does so and then stretches out full length on her back staring up at the trees. Student sits beside her, watching her. Time passes.)
Ross:	(to Student[2]) What's happening?
Student[2]:	The wind has got up now and the blossom is showering down. I want to leap up!

Throughout this piece the rest of the group was watching: a perceptible atmosphere grew as the "action" developed and we already sensed something intense and exciting in the air between these two women. My role was simply to help the idea grow by sensing image-making possibilities. We were free when the piece was over to discuss its quality, its meaning, the skills of the makers and performers. Whatever we liked. Converting it into a score for performance by others would have been another equally valid possibility. I like this way of working very much because it keeps me close to what is happening without its becoming my idea; however, my imagination is free to work directly and immediately in response to the dramatic displacement occurring before me and I become imaginatively useful to my students.

On the next occasion with this group a very strange story began to unfold in and around a Hansel and Gretel type house in the forest. I had simply said to one of a mixed group of children and adults, "Do you see this room?". We had previously warmed up by working in pairs as stereotypes; each actor improvising a character to go with one of the words of a pair: Bright and Breezy; Dust and Ashes; Free and Easy: Fast and Loose; Down and Out (Shades of Hinge and Bracket, Cannon and Ball etc etc). We found after a while that the house in the wood was lived in by a woman alone and was being visited by a rather odd succession of people. Was it sheer chance that the woman playing the lead had been Down in the pair Down and Out? A young child (Free) had strayed into the garden on an impulse, the point or character of which was yet unclear. Then, after a brief encounter between these two, they were joined by a rather sinister man who, in the warm-up session, had taken the part of Out. I then suggested that the rest of the group might look in at the windows of the house – each framed an enigmatic face. Dust, Ashes. And Fast. The woman opened one of the windows and pleaded with Fast to go away. "Yes, certainly", he replied obligingly. But he didn't move. Then Breezy blew the door shut! In discussion the following week we began to sense the scenario for an anti-nuclear fairy-story in all this, and were excited and somewhat surprised by the bizarre, quite coincidental fit between the warm-up exercise and the improvisation itself. The original story was drawn from a teenage girl who then stood aside to allow an older woman, more suited to the role she had created, to take over as protagonist – but the girl continued to compose at my side, watching the action grow.

What need of "themes" and "topics" when we all have so much at our imaginative fingertips! For the teacher inclined to work this way it is simply a matter of knowing what kind of thing you are after, the *quality* of response you are looking for, and then of establishing the conditions (essentially safety i.e. privacy) in which there is a strong chance of the right kind of thing occurring. And always the quality of the thing is a factor of individual engagement, of the absorption or occupation of those whose form it is. The more skilful and experienced the group becomes in generating ideas (musical, literary, visual, dramatic) the more subtle and more satisfying will their expressive actions become. And the generating of ideas is absolutely bound up with the ability to use and to control the medium, an essential element of which is understanding the conventions by which it achieves expressive form.

I always evaluate the work in terms of imaginative verve and flair, but also of medium control. The craft of art quickly becomes a vital factor in expressive performance and I never find a group that has been involved in this kind of composition uninterested in the "technical" and "perceptual" expertise or lack of expertise that the work has disclosed. Such evaluation that concentrates upon form and forming, rather than on content, be it social, moral or anything else, is the only absolutely necessary evaluation. Discussion of the life-issues raised and the insights achieved is of course entirely relevant to any discussion of art since art invariably draws upon and feeds back into "life". However, my prime concern is with the artifice, the artifact. The criteria of aesthetic evaluation are aesthetic — which is to say concerned with sensibility.

Assessment and evaluation are, of course, part of the "attending" function: when we recreate or realize a form in our own imagination by "reading" the clues provided in a composition we inevitably judge its quality at the same time as we read its character and discover its meaning. Our matrix of aesthetic action is a ready-made formula for assessment. We decide whether we are assessing the composition, that is to say, the thing formed, or its interpretation in performance or both. We then work down the aesthetic elements focusing on each in turn. We might decide to ignore some and concentrate upon others. I worked with an adult group recently that was attempting an evaluation of a musical improvisation which they had tape-recorded as it was being created. They were interested to discover something about the way they worked from the evidence available. It was agreed that the piece should be assessed first of all purely descriptively in terms of instrumental balance and a monitoring procedure was evolved that entailed marking the piece for balance at intervals of thirty seconds.

30 secs	1	2	3	4	5	6	7	8	9	10	11	12	13	14	15	16
Flute	3	3	3	3	3	3	3	3	3	3	3	3	3	2	—	3
Xylophone	—	1	—	1	1	1	1	1	—	—	—	—	1	2	—	—
Piano	3	2	2	1	1	1	3	3	2	2	2	2	2	2	2	2
Percussion	—	—	1	—	1	1	—	—	1	2	2	3	2	2	2	1

As the piece was played back one member of the group signalled the moment of assessment and everyone marked each instrument for relative dominance on a three-point scale:

From this analysis a discussion developed around a variety of topics. The dominance of the flute was not simply remarked but questioned: the piece was clearly an accompanied solo for most of the time – and the group debated whether this was in fact the best solution to the problem it had set itself. What about the reticence of the xylophone throughout? The player in question confessed to feeling uninvolved and that had actually meant that the piece was largely developed without that feature. There seemed to be a reasonable balance struck between the other instruments after moment 8 and up to about 14. Just listening to the tape made it clear that the musical idea didn't actually materialize until some four minutes had elapsed and was exhausted after a further three minutes. Moment 12 seemed the most balanced.

We then decided to listen for the emergence of the idea and see how this related to instrumental balance – sensing that balance was as much a creative as an aesthetic factor (i.e. related to the inter-action of individual minds and not simply a question of sound quality). The group's assessment of coherence was as follows – individuals A, B, C, and D.

30 secs	1	2	3	4	5	6	7	8	9	10	11	12	13	14	15	16
A	0	1	1	2	2	2	3	3	3	2	3	3	3	2	2	2
B	1	1	2	2	2	2	3	3	3	3	3	3	3	2	2	2
C	1	1	1	1	1	2	2	3	2	1	1	2	3	1	2	1
D	1	3	3	3	3	3	3	3	3	3	3	3	3	3	3	3

From looking at the general level of agreement amongst the members of the group it would appear that there were essentially two "periods" of real coherence: between 6 and 9 and 12 and 13. A and B clearly saw the piece as gradually achieving coherence around 6 and sustaining it until around 13 after which it seemed rather to peter out. D wasn't really sure how to understand the exercise and maintained that in his terms it all made interesting listening! C drew attention to 10 and 11 where he felt there was a loss of concentration among the players – a lapse of what he called "perceptual" sensitivity. He detected a decomposition of the idea at that point. A had clearly had some misgivings too (10) and a further listening to that section led to general agreement with C's assessment.

These are instances, taken more or less at random, of a fairly systematic approach to appraising or receiving as a way of promoting and informing an objective evaluation of what was initially a very private and essentially transient experience. The technique was certainly justified in terms of the quality of the discussion and of the critical attention it facilitated. However it was generally agreed that although such an analysis might have a great deal to offer in the context of musical discourse and understanding, it did absolutely nothing for the actual musical experience of listening imaginatively. In that respect we had had very much more success with a different technique. On that occasion we had listened to the first 10 seconds of a piece of recorded music (Mahler's Third Symphony First Movement) and then written down our impressions; our feelings, the images evoked and so forth. We rather discouraged guesses as to dating and the name of the composer etc, though not technical descriptions of what was going on in the music. We continued the assessment by listening to an increasing amount of the passage – 20 seconds, 30 seconds, 40 seconds, 60 seconds, 120 seconds etc, each time beginning at the beginning and noting our feelings and such perceptual changes as we were aware of. The results were fascinating in two respects: in the first place we felt we had been listening with very great concentration, really dwelling in the music as well as dwelling upon it (another instance of "occupation"); secondly we felt absolutely compelled to find out "what happened next" – just as if we had been listening to a story or watching a drama.

Much good discourse followed that served only to intensify and enrich the imaginative experience itself. We later made pictures – graphic "impressions" – of the total character of the piece we had heard. The effect of this final exercise was to focus upon our musical and affective memories so as to evoke the impulse needed to give coherence to the mark making. I think we had strayed into, or perhaps moved on to, the "mediating" role. But then our verbal interpretations had been just such acts of mediation. Perhaps the simplest way of separating "attending" from "mediating" is to see the latter as expressive (as I have already said, as something akin to performance) in that it involves the presentation of aesthetic appraisal as both an account of what happens (i.e. a description of what seems to be there together with a record of its effect upon the receiver) and a judgement as to its quality. Whereas simply "attending" asks no externalization of response – simply discriminative engagement with the form. These distinctions become important when as teachers we wish to assess our students' performances in these four different roles.

These two or three instances are sufficient I think to make clear the close inter-connectedness between the four aesthetic roles we have identified and the way in which one can ring the changes between conscious and unconscious processes and outward and inward directed attention. Each teacher develops his or her own technique for getting forming, performing, attending and mediating going. There are no definitive practices either in art or in arts education. There are however absolutely definite criteria of relevant achievement. What matters for the purposes of this essay is that we agree upon these criteria, upon the respective value of each operational function, and more particularly that we see them rooted in a single-minded commitment to develop and enhance sensibility as the means of individual psychic integration. I really don't think I need go on instancing ways of working in media such as words and movement and colour and line merely in order to give this account a greater claim to comprehensiveness. It is after all the *principles* underlying the practice that it is the purpose of this essay to bring out.

CHAPTER 13

Assessing Aesthetic Development

If aesthetic education seeks the qualification of sensibility how are we to conceive of aesthetic development and how to go about assessing children's progress? These two related issues highlight more than any others the soft-centre of the arts curriculum today. The ideas of Gardner, Erikson, Kohlberg and Parsons are considered and a speculative model is offered that proposes qualitative differences aligned with the maturation of sensibility and identifies four phases of aesthetic development: the age of displacement, the age of improvisation, the age of convention and the age of formal abstraction.

★   ★   ★   ★   ★

Despite the use of the term "development" in the title of the APU undertaking in the aesthetic area, the topic was found to be so contentious as continually to frustrate conclusive discussion. Which means that the Group's final report gives it no mention at all. Aesthetic "development" receives one paragraph in the Gulbenkian Foundation's report *The Arts in Schools*, barely ten lines. Nothing to the point is said – in fact the paragraph is notable for expressing an essentially non-developmental view of arts education.

> "Not to attempt at some stage, and in some form, to involve children in the arts is simply to fail to educate them as fully developed, intelligent and feeling human beings." (Page 20)

The inference surely to be drawn from this statement is that attempts to involve children in the arts may be equally well made at any stage and in any form – it matters not when or in which. And I would doubt very much whether such a view would find much support amongst, for example, the teachers of the arts. I suspect, even without having the benefit of a clearly articulated model of aesthetic development to refer to, most arts teachers are not only aware that children's needs and capacities change but actually attempt to accommodate those changes within their curriculum plans. And, of course, there is ample literature to support the general thesis of development within the aesthetic area: it just doesn't seem in the least sensible to suggest that doing work in drama when you are seven would compensate for not doing any painting when you were fifteen.

The point of taking the idea of development seriously would in fact be to hit this notion of the once-for-all "baptismal" or "innoculation" approach pretty firmly on the head. If you hold that developmental changes are discernible in children's aesthetic responses and that, for all that they have in common, the impact of experience in one art form is not transferable to nor alternatively available in another art form, then the case for a continuing and wide ranging education in the arts is irresistible. Whereas if you are of the Gulbenkian persuasion you are much less of a burden to and so can be more easily accommodated within the traditional curriculum. I hope it is obvious enough not to need much by way of further explanation that I hold firmly to the developmental view myself and, despite the damaging shortage of hard information about the mechanics of the process or even about the criteria that would reliably indicate excellence of performance, would expect to teach if not with explicit then at least with implicit principles in mind.

On the issue of aesthetic "maturity" Ernest Goodman (in Ross, 1981) provides an interesting and, given his considerable experience, what must amount to an authoritative table of factors which would apply to work in the visual arts. I daresay we could all have a reasonable shot at providing such a checklist for achievement in our own subject areas – and might indeed go further to begin grouping "levels" in relation to either chronological age or some model of aesthetic development however naive or tentative. Undoubtedly much work needs urgently to be done – not least amongst teachers themselves who are probably the richest repository of experience in this field.

The main difficulty lies in the fact that, for whatever reason, arts teachers are not used to thinking "developmentally" – in the sense of working to some systematic procedure that links effective problem handling in the classroom with some reasonably coherent scheme of the development of sensibility. It surely goes without saying that we need some notion of development to give credibility and authority to our curriculum practice – at the most rudimentary level we shall want to be able to anticipate why a particular task or why specific material that would go down well in one situation might be totally inappropriate in another. Further than that however we need some coherent ideas about development if we are to make any sense of the idea of progress in a child's work: our criteria of progress will help to indicate development. What is sobering to say the least is to discover how exceptional is any discussion of this issue and associated issues among teachers themselves. Very recently I have detected some interest in this area in connection with the discussion about joint examining at 16+: I am certain that we have to begin by pooling what we know and then try to systematize what we are to look for.

A difficulty that arises when we begin to think about development concerns the scope or range of our interest. From our curriculum model presented earlier it must be immediately clear that many different kinds of development will materially affect a child's successful aesthetic maturation. Howard Gardner (1973) in his book *The Arts and Human Development* focuses upon three interacting systems of feeling, perceiving and making as constituting development in the arts. In particular he makes use of the work of Freud and of Eric Erikson – particularly the latter's account of emotional development presented in *Childhood and Society*: Gardner also, pretty obviously, draws on Piaget's model of conceptual development. His own particular contribution concerns the notion of symbolic development and he concludes that, given what it takes to be a user of iconic symbols, most children have all the basic equipment of the artist by the time they are seven-years-old.

There are few other such focused studies in this area that I have been able to discover, with the notable exception of the work of Michael Parsons and his associates. Parsons examines children's verbal responses to paintings in terms of a model of aesthetic development that in some respects tallies closely with Kohlberg's account of moral development. In short, Parsons discerns three basic levels of development which coincide approximately with Kohlberg's pre-conventional, conventional and post-conventional stages. Children moving from a very egocentric perception of the meaning of art objects through a concern for the rules of conventions governing art to an engagement with the expressive and aesthetic quality of works of art as elements in their own right. To what extent this entirely verbal and hence discursive material can be held to yield significant information as to aesthetic responsiveness is at least open to some question and although the attitudes of children to aesthetic practice are one important dimension of aesthetic development it may not be felt that such attitudes inferred from verbal accounts are either of the greatest relevance where sensibility is concerned or could be adapted for other uses – as in the response to music or drama (which, be it said, Parsons makes no claim for).

Aesthetic development will be a factor of many different developments, psychological, mental, emotional, cultural, and any diagnosis the object of which might be a corrective or remedial programme would have to take account of all these inter-acting factors. Our criteria of sensibility provide some clues as to the lines upon which an assessment might be based however, as well as indicating fields for further investigation.

Level 1. *Pragmatic Attention*:
Coherence: essentially a perceptual operation. The principal criterion that we have assigned to Level 1 makes claims upon the powers of perception, discrimination and whatever store we might set upon a purely intuitive

feeling for coherences – the basic principle investigated by Eysenck (in Ross, 1983) in his Visual Aesthetic Sensitivity Test.

Level 2.   *Disinterested Attention*:
Uniqueness: here the quality of disinterestedness impinges upon aesthetic judgement and the object is appraised "in its own right" – as particular. Again several faculties are at work, not least one's acquaintance with the "field" in which the evaluation is being made, for who is to distinguish between the unique and the stereotype who has no acquaintance with the species of the objects under review? Furthermore, as the label "detachment" suggests, the appreciation of uniqueness calls for a special type of attention and this is as much an affective as it is a mental operation.
Fit: the "informed" dimension of aesthetic judgement – knowing what counts.
Authenticity: our sense that the work is honest, has integrity, commitment.

Level 3.   *Tacit Attention*:
Multi-dimensionality or openness: is the product of certain qualities of personality and is intrinsically bound up with "metaphor and ambiguity."
Empathy: the ability to identify personal meaning, to get feeling into sensuous forms lies at the very heart of the artistic response and is likely to be composite of mental and emotional resources. For instance we have to feel free to invest forms with feeling, to give vent or play to the imagination, and there will be those children whose emotional instability will leave them very apprehensive and intolerant of the kinds of stress that sometimes attend projective action.

There is no suggestion absolutely that the levels themselves are developmentally achieved, that children will mature from Level 1 through Level 2 to Level 3. Rather, we shall find children operating at all three levels but that their operations will be qualitatively different – as with, for example, my suggestion concerning modes of representation or symboling. We already know a good deal about the changes discernible in children's visual artwork – rather less about their music and drama and story telling – though even here there is increasing interest being shown by researchers. We also know from the work of Lawrence Kohlberg something about the way children's capacities to make moral judgements develop. I have already discussed (Ross, 1981) the possible implications of Kohlberg's theory of moral maturity for aesthetic education. Michael Parsons and his associates (D'Onofrio and Nodine) have adopted and adapted Kohlberg's (and through him, Piaget's) principles in assessing children's verbal appreciation of visual works of art.
   I approach the issue of aesthetic development itself by asking questions about people's possible artistic motivation, on the assumption that anything

one might say about the arts will inevitably incorporate what one might also wish to say about the perception of coherence and the feeling for quality. It seems reasonable to say that where the drive or impulse to make or encounter art is concerned, there are at least three distinguishable types of reward that might be significant in affecting motivation. Which is another way of saying that art meets human needs in at least three identifiable ways: these are

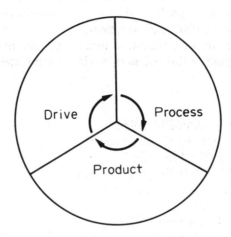

"process" rewards, "drive" rewards and "product" rewards. Motivating artwork at any level means giving equal consideration to arousing, releasing and harnessing drive, to resourcing and assisting process, and to helping in the satisfactory achievement and appraisal of artistic products.

Processing is not enough:

> without drive it is purposeless, mere going through the motions.
> Without successful product it remains unresolved.

Product is not enough:

> without drive it has no meaning, it is a sham. Without intrinsically valued process it is just labour – not a labour of love.

Drive is not enough:

> without effective process there can be no resolution and without a satisfactory product there is only frustration and repression.

Here are some of the rewards that art participators might be looking for:

Drive

Desire to react expressively to experience, to try to give feelings a coherent and objective (symbolic) form, to find meaning in our creative, imaginative inventions and by our own efforts.

Desire for stimulus: to experience the world and one's being more intensely, to respond emotionally and sensually, to feel involved, particularly to experience life as valuable and significant, funny, ugly, good.

Desire to communicate one's ideas and feelings to others, to share, to be at one with, to find fellowship and make common cause, to contribute.

Desire to capture, seize, record, preserve, show – to cherish and secure for whatever purpose, to recover what otherwise might be lost.

Drive to leave or make one's mark, to assert oneself, present oneself, to alter, change, enhance, disfigure, transfigure.

Desire to analyse and understand, to probe, explore, investigate.

Desire to participate in the visionary world – for inscape, for poetry.

Process

Decoration

Manipulation and handling of media

Exercise of skills and their enhancement
   through instruction and practice

Engagement with a problem, concentration

Being imaginative, inventive and creative

Surprise and discovery

Making to order, following a design

Working with materials and people

Dreaming and reverie

Feeling alive, intense, alert, active, concentrated

Embodying personal significance

Product

The self actualized, manifested, realized

Insight achieved (coherence out of chaos)

Something useful to oneself

Something useful to others

An objective accomplished successfully

Increased self esteem

Time transcended

Extrinsic rewards obtained

Significance embodied

The placing of something good in the world

Given that all intelligent action is tied to such reward systems I have asked myself in what way it might be possible to schematize the rewards associated with the arts activities of infants, children and adults. It seemed to me that this might be one way of creating a developmental model that could be tested experientially if not actually experimentally – maybe that too. I concluded that we might be able to group artistic responses and satisfactions into four broad categories ranging from the most elementary to the most sophisticated and that these categories might be useful in drawing up both general criteria of assessment in the arts and also for considering curricular contents and objectives. I have speculated about development in Art, Drama and Music: if these profiles are found to have some substance then it would not I think be difficult to adapt the scheme to other aesthetic areas.

Development in Art
1. (years 0–2) Pure sensuous engagement with materials – simple "displacement". The beginnings of expression. Continuity and immediacy rather than abstraction: patterning, ordering and manipulation.
2. (years 3–7) Perception of "mark" as the outcome of interaction with materials – displacement as signifier, as *representative* of experience. Leads to depiction of the object world as known rather than as seen and the playful manipulation of experience through a simple act of abstraction. Visual marks are manipulated in much the same way as toys and other objects – as part of mastery play. Imagination is at a premium allowing the constant elaboration, extension and adaptation of the abstracted, marked world at the behest of the need to order and develop the world of feeling. Imaginative forms are *improvised*. In Piagetian terms assimilation is dominant. The young child recognizes an affinity between drawing and writing, both use marks as a code.
3. (years 8–13) Perception of the representative as potentially *representational*, that is to say as corresponding visually with the object world. The *conventions* of artistic representation now become of interest and their mastery of concern to the child. This perception of the art process as a set of conventions coincides with a shift of interest away from the more self-centred, assimilation-dominated character of imaginative play towards an increasing concern with the adult's world, with "reality", with the need to become significant and viable in a world that is subject to rules hitherto unrealized. At this stage the symbol receives its validity from the object to which it refers. There is perhaps a diminution of imaginative and inventive activity in the interests of producing artifacts that meet conventional criteria; however there is a limit to the satisfactions obtainable in the mere mastery of conventional image-making practices and a motivational problem arises if the forms produced cease to correlate with inner states, cease to satisfy expressive needs – needs which are nonetheless insistent for all this new affective concern with *impressive* mental strategies. The art teacher has at least three principal tasks at this time: (1) to instruct the child in the conventions of artistic representations (2) to help the child to "see" – to improve vision (3) to keep expressive impulse at the centre of the image

making. You might add a 4th – to maintain contact with the purely sensuous and the improvisatory activities of the earlier stages of development.

4. (14+) Perception of the representational symbol as significant in its own right – as *presentational* or iconic; that sensuous forms embody meanings intrinsically and are not tied referentially to stand for objects in the world. The "poetic" symbol systems are autonomous meaning-systems capable of an infinite range of signification and open to the individual to order and exploit for any communicative purpose. The child becomes aware that art is a language – but a very special kind of language: that sensuous forms may carry the most profound meanings of which man is capable. This application lends a different emphasis to the interest in convention, which now comes, above all else, the means to the expression or realization of a personal vision. Image is constructed on the principle of inner coherence and perception becomes or recovers its holistic character. The integrity of the art form is a matter now not so much of improvisation or of taking impressions from the object world as of *composition* – of the artifact's independent and inner coherence. Particularly of the integration of form and feeling ("frame and content" – Polanyi). This is the stage of pure symbolic operation – of full aesthetic maturity – in which the infant's simple enthusiasm for displacement becomes an act of pure signification; expression and convention are one. Style becomes the man. Again there are special problems for the teacher: (1) to ensure that the perception of pure presentational symbol occurs and is reinforced – i.e. that the transition from impression to composition is secured (2) to encourage the development of a personal style whilst extending the child's appreciation of artistic conventions (3) maintaining the centrality of impulse and the integrity of the expressive drive (4) ensuring continuing contact with the earlier strategies of improvisation and impression. In some ways it is true to say that to become a mature artist you have to recover something of the spontaneity and naivety of the infant – that Phase 4 is in some ways most like Phase 1. But we look above all for the presence and power of a personal vision.

Drama

1. (years 0–2) Pure sensuous engagement with materials – physical displacement and gesture.
2. (years 3–7) Perception of gesture as expressive, displacement as signifier. Expressive gestures (of voice as well as of body) are incorporated into make-believe play where situations representative of personal encounters and happenings in the object world are simulated and

re-enacted as part of the process of subjective integration. Objects are drawn into dramatic play and situations enacted as in a puppet theatre with the child as puppeteer. No undue attention is given to verisimilitude: events are developed spontaneously and with absolute subservience to the psychic need of the moment. Children quickly discover the value of acting with another child – and of collaborative "puppet" work. Conventions (e.g. words substituting for otherwise unrealizable effects or events – rather like stage directions, sound effects etc) are idiosyncratic. Roles are assumed and changed and swapped with equal readiness. Dressing-up is more a matter of equipping the actor with what is felt to be an authorizing emblem than with any concern, for instance, for illusion. Non-identification between actor and part, though deep commitment to the imaginative world created in the play. *Improvisation* is the key skill. Thorough involvement with imaginative role-play at this stage will help prevent the loss of confidence in projection that sometimes attends adolescence. Drama is instrumental to learning at this stage of development. Inhibitions are at their lowest.

3. (years 8–13) Greater concern with the forms and conventions of real-life drama – interest in film and television as "models" and as source material. Desire to be true-to-life, to take scenes and issues from the real world and make their own versions conform to reality rather than simply acting as the vehicles of impulse. Awareness of acting skills and lack of such skills becomes an inhibiting factor for the first time. The issues and effects are perceived melodramatically and sentimentally. Role play, simulation and documentary become popular forms: the satisfaction now comes from creating dramas that are like professional dramas and that deal with "real" events in the world. Mise-en-scène acquires significance and mere fantasy and improvisation begin to lose their appeal. The drama is dominated by story – which must have coherence and consistency and must end significantly. The great danger at this time lies in the adoption of stock material and the subservience to cliché. Taking and creating right *impressions* is what this stage seems to be all about.

4. (14+) The drama becomes a personal expressive form – dramatic forms are symbolic statements in their own right, not simply imitations of scenes from life. The form becomes more fluid and more experimental – no longer bound to traditional stereotype. The young actors become aware of the special relationship between their real feelings and personalities and those of the characters they are portraying. One of the appeals of drama becomes the scope it offers for affective projection and exploration, whereas for some children the onset of adolescence brings uncertainty and selfconsciousness that severely inhibit the "expressive" use of gesture. Drama is a physical medium and for many

children in adolescence, physical selfconsciousness can put a severe restriction upon freedom of movement and interpersonal action. Selfconsciousness becomes the burden that attends a new degree of self-awareness. Story-line is less dominant and character interest goes along with a concern for the complexity of the issues and tensions that bind people into dramatic relationships. The coherence of the overall structure (character and action) is more important than episode or caricature: we have reached the stage of dramatic *composition* and of the pure dramatic symbol – of drama as a symbolic act of significance in its own right. The above account is not intended to imply spontaneous achievement. It may very well require considerable skills on the part of the drama teacher to bring the kind of perceptions I have just listed into being.

Music

1. (years 0–2) Pure sensuous engagement with sound materials – simple displacement and discrimination. Experimentation and recognition, solace in relating a sensuous structure to a feeling or mood. Absorption and surrender.

2. (years 3–7) Tune perceived as an aural phenomenon (pitch and rhythmic structure – i.e. sound in time and space) and then used improvisationally to accompany, and give structure to other more specifically focused activities, such as movement sequences, dramatic games etc. Musical doodling, particularly vocal doodling, is a feature of expression at this stage. Practice is of the essence, leading to the tuning of the ear and progressive mastery of sound structures and patterns. Musical memory develops. Much unconscious conventional assimilation and induction proceeds at this time. Being musical means, among other things, being able to anticipate musical developments and events on the basis of presented cues or clues. A period of unselfconscious experimentation and delight in which the powers of anticipation develop. Music as stimulus to fantasy: sounds as sound effects.

3. (years 8–13) Concern with the conventions of musical production and predilection for creating and hearing the right (i.e. harmonic) sounds. Desire to join the adult scene, to know about adult (not to be confused with classical) music and musicians, to develop a taste for the experience of music as symbolic of a desired way of life, as conferring membership of a desired social group. Programme or narrative and descriptive music makes sense. Desire to become conventionally proficient, to learn an instrument and especially thereby to emulate an idol. Capacity for grasping simple musical structures fully developed. As with the other arts a motivational crisis occurs if competence and expressive impulse do not remain productively aligned. The child must

be able to use the conventions of music to express himself – music must make sense, must have meaning, even within what are likely to be rather rigid and constricted notions of what is acceptable. Signature music in all its forms – music as referential sign – predominates. Pastiche, imitations and reproductions are all popular devices at this time: this is the *impressive* period of musical development. Teachers must (1) satisfy the demand for greater conventional competence (2) keep music close to expression and feeling (3) allow scope for the satisfaction of "impressive" needs.

4. (14+) Perception of music as a form of communication and language of personal expression – as embodying meaning and vision (an individual's, a group's, a people's). Musical *compositions* become "symbolic" structures – the possibility of personal style, as composer and performer, and of personal taste as listener emerges strongly. The mature musician is able to progress from simple (discrete) to complex (holistic) perception, and tolerance of ambiguity and inconclusiveness develops. Quality becomes a significant concern – and music becomes a purely formal delight rather than merely serving as an emblem or programme. It is no longer adequately paraphrased but operates directly and within its own system of signification. All the previously acquired skills of discrimination, of encoding and decoding, now come into their own in the pursuit of the transcendental, the visionary, the personally expressive. The earlier devotion with pop broadens to include a developing taste for more complex and more progressive forms; complex classical works take over from the simpler pieces of programme or narrative music; a readiness to approach unfamiliar works in whatever idiom manifests itself. Teachers will (1) feed the growing capacity to handle more complex musical forms (2) encourage the development of personal style and taste (3) reinforce all the earlier skills and experiences so that they may be incorporated into this final and most mature phase.

A full account of aesthetic development in schools would mean considering the three levels of sensibility: the cognitive, the effective and the "poetic", in terms of each of the four stages I have proposed above. For convenience I have labelled the four phases

1. Displacement
2. Improvisation
3. Convention
4. Composition

What is to be done pending the testing and authorization or modification of this model? Well, obviously, where assessment is concerned, we go on working intuitively – but perhaps more sensitive to the kinds of issues raised in this chapter and, in particular, to the need for greater objectivity in our descriptions of what children are doing. As Maloney (in Ross, 1981) suggests, the best way forward in the area of aesthetic assessment would seem to be to marry *informed subjective judgement* with good *objective description*. And on the developmental issue, I doubt very much whether any model will do more than suggest ways in which we might be able to compensate for the breakdown of what ought, under normal circumstances, to be spontaneous, organic growth.

The excuse most frequently cited for most of the more extravagant excesses of educational practice is the need for a speeded up or accelerated induction of children into conventional ways of thinking and of acquiring knowledge. Although we might very well feel that children can learn a good deal about the conventions governing the practices of art through formal instruction, I would certainly wish to see the basic emphasis of aesthetic development given over to spontaneous and natural growth and the last thing that seems to me to be appropriate to development in this particular field is any notion of accelerated learning. We don't need to jet-propel children's sensibilities. We can do a lot worse than allow that our decisions about the kinds of making and attending experiences to which children should be exposed should be governed by common-sense. We have, I think, a perfect example of spontaneous aesthetic development in children's play and it is absurd to wish to speed up or short-circuit their experience of play. This is surely one area of human development where we must protect the natural growth of the species whilst recognizing that it is entirely "natural" for man the sign-maker to become culturally adapted. The greatest service we can render children will be in freeing them to go on developing and in protecting their developing sensibility from distortion and premature demise. And that means providing conditions of safety and encouragement, supplying them with the resources and the skills they need, stimulating imagination when it flags, helping them believe in themselves and in the aesthetic dimension of their own being.

All these provisions will help to supply the freedom they need, and freedom is what they need. The crisis of the adolescent develops out of the loss of media-freedom that childhood meant, and the sense of powerlessness to achieve the freedom with media of adulthood. This he knows to be what he now most desires. And so, for a while – perhaps for ever – he is lost on the threshold of adulthood, mesmerized by a burgeoning sense of possibility and seemingly equipped to achieve nothing at all. It is certainly my own experience, working with relatively inhibited young children and adults, that once they feel their strength, once they realize that they can trust themselves, trust their hunches and intuitions – that the experience of a good-enough childhood, with its freedoms of playing, imagining, feeling and forming is a precious legacy upon which to build a flourishing and creative adulthood –

they readily acquire the techniques and assimilate the conventions that their new personalities demand for their expression.

I spent almost three years as a member of the Aesthetic Group of the Assessment of Performance Unit at the DES and I think my only significant contribution – at least I feel it to have been so – was to be one of those arguing most forcefully *against* any decision to go ahead with a programme of national monitoring. Most of my other, possibly more positive suggestions, like for instance keeping to the original concept of "aesthetic" and not confining ourselves to a discussion of the arts, did not find acceptance. I am now rather clearer than I was at the time why I wanted to resist any national programme of assessment. I just cannot see what sort of information that sampled aesthetic "performance" across the country could be seen as affording a really significant picture of what was going on in the school system. And then the aesthetic, as we have seen, finds its significance in embodiment as particularity – and particularity as a quality is, I would have thought, irreducible to general principles.

> "Association of content and frame is an integration that produces its own incomparable, purely imaginative experience – an experience that can be judged by no external criteria – and we should like to make such imaginative experience the cornerstone of aesthetic theory." (Polanyi and Prosch 1976)

So very much should I but whether or not it were actually possible to monitor national standards of children's so-called aesthetic performance it would surely be entirely undesirable to do so because it would be objectionable in principle – as another example of what Marcuse calls "the rule and the power of the whole". The aesthetic above all is idiosyncratic, unpredictable, local and spontaneous. The effect of the publication of national "results" and the possible league-tabling of schools (as in the USA) on aesthetic grounds would clearly be a monumental disaster for aesthetic education in this country, permitting the usurpation of "communitas" by "status" (see Preface). National monitoring we are assured is entirely painless – would go almost unnoticed by those involved and would do no actual harm to the children comprising the random sample. Rather like being a blood-donor, except that giving blood might be of real significance to someone else whereas giving or yielding an aesthetic statistic is more than likely to be of no use to anyone.

On the more general subject of assessment in the arts I am always brought up short by this warning of Carl Rogers (in Vernon, 1970).

> "Evaluation is always a threat, always creates a need for defensiveness, always means that some portion of experience must be denied to awareness".

There has to be a sense in which the threat of evaluation is a very serious one and yet, as I hope some of what I have said already might suggest, it may not be altogether entirely avoidable and given the right context could be formative and valuable. I would go further and say that I should not balk at assessing my students on some such grounds as my matrix suggests – recognizing that the criteria by which one would assess, say, "coherence" or "uniqueness" or "projective power" would differ from one art form to another and would need to be very carefully worked out. But I suspect such a task would be well within the competence of anyone with some training in or feeling for art, or music, or drama or dance or literature. Associated fields such as RE, PE and CDT, would have their own criteria. I myself feel pretty convinced that

(1) There must be continuous evaluation by students and teachers of aesthetic education.

(2) That students need to be able to make up their own minds about the quality of their work and the work of others and enter into public discourse on both issues.

(3) That aesthetic responses can be "objectively" assessed as more or less imaginative, more or less sensitive, more or less sophisticated.

(4) That teachers should be prepared to assess the competence of their pupils and make these assessments available to the students and to such other persons who might reasonably claim an interest in them. I don't see that such an involvement offends against Rogers' concern for "unconditional positive regard"; correcting an error or recognizing a fault or an inability in someone you care about is not the same as withdrawing favour.

(5) That all forms of competitiveness in the aesthetic area are to be discouraged as likely to corrupt sensibility and destroy conviviality – hence that most forms of public examination, normatively referenced, would have to be outlawed.

Convivial assessment is an idea I owe to Christopher Beedell (in Ross, 1981). He voices his suspicion of the APU exercise in the following terms:

"Artistic expression ... is basically a collective enterprise. I think that collective is made up of the maker, those from whom the maker has learnt and the maker's audience. It is that 'constituency' which the maker trusts in order to have the courage to undertake the making, and it is that constituency which the maker trusts to evaluate what is made.... What is 'manipulative' and false to the process of making is the attempt to represent the collective by *replacing* it with external assessors. To do that is to gobble up the meaning of the made."

Beedell seems to be warning us against allowing our assessment practice to vitiate the populist principles which we have already said are the right and the only pre-conditions of good work in the aesthetic realm of education. And I would not want to demur.

What particularly attracts me, however, to the notion of a "convivial" assessment is what I sense to be a very deep-seated need amongst makers of all things whatsoever to "share" what they have made in the sense of carrying outside into the light of everyday what began as an inchoate personal response to experience. And Beedell's comments seem to me to be the last word on all forms of external assessment in arts education. It is often suggested that the urge to rush off with what we have done and show it to somebody is a sign that we are somehow uncertain of its actual worth ourselves and so require some kind of reassurance in the matter. Such an attitude is certainly widespread in education and is the direct consequence of subservience to external assessment. I read this urge slightly differently. When we present what we have done for the appraisal of another we are forced to reassess it ourselves: we often choose as the first assessor someone whose "positive regard" we know we can rely on. Which means we don't risk loss of face or esteem should the work be appraised as flawed. I find a connection between the notion of the good-enough mother (the eternal companion of all our good-playing) and the good-enough assessor. We need to detach ourselves from what we have done before we can genuinely appraise it, and that act whereby we present it to another makes such detachment a psychological fact and assists the only really significant form of assessment in the aesthetic area, that is to say self-assessment.

But I think there is something more besides. A work unshared somehow remains barren, unfulfilled, suffocated. We sense somehow that until what has been a largely subjective experience is impregnated with objectivity it remains unconsummated: ideas and objects must be released into the world to take their place within and help to fructify and fertilize the system. From that moment they have a destiny of their own and we can relinquish our "interest" in them – in fact we often do lose interest at just that point and that is probably as it should be. What is wrong with an evaluation that is tied to a system of extrinsic rewards, penalties, qualifications and disqualifications is that it somehow invalidates the whole essence and direction of the creative thrust which is towards release, distance, giving, yielding up, letting go in the spirit of conviviality. Or as a young friend put it to me recently of "placing something good in the world". It is the same with all our experiences of the spontaneous and the transcendent: the desire above all things to have someone share something inherently good with us. I sense that such a desire springs from this deeply rooted sense we have that the inner life must be granted, an "external destiny". It is this impulse that provides the touchstone for all our discussion of assessment and evaluation in the aesthetic area. It is one way of participating in the sacred ritual of the exchange of gifts.

In practice of course we must see aesthetic assessment within the wider context of school assessment as a whole and then we immediately find ourself confronting the familiar and awesome dilemma: whether to seek legitimacy through a closer identification between the artistic and main-stream education's commitment to the academic values enshrined in the public examination system, or whether by repudiating the system to run the undoubted risk of being written off as essentially beyond the pale, as literally extra-curricular. It is a very real dilemma and a decision either way is fraught with danger; I don't want to cast any stones – particularly as I can really see no ready or clear solution. On the face of it it is asking an awful lot to have one's work evaluated fairly by an establishment whose central values you disparage and reject: the only reasonable thing for someone in that predicament to do would be in some sense to withdraw from the system altogether – perhaps by conceding that aesthetic education is something for after or outside normal schooling. And yet such a position is one very few of us are prepared to adopt because in the first place we are committed to the principle of an education "for life" rather than education as training in a limited range of skills, and in the second place we feel that education in the hands of a teaching force more or less completely devoted to academic and vocational goals would be a seriously distorted group in the sense that there would be no voices urging the imaginative principle and no lives committed to its manifestation and demonstration. This for me is one of the principal dangers of the impact of the present programme of cuts in education.

What we must do, obviously, is to restrict the distortion of and imbalance in educational thinking by every means available to us, and not least by entering into the public debate on the future of education with clear arguments informed by understanding. In addition we must lose no oppor-tunity of demonstrating the effectiveness and relevance of the work we do. As for assessment, it seems to me that we have to work very hard to find suitable ways of accounting for what we do and of ascertaining and indicating children's in-school aesthetic progress in a non-competitive form. We must also enter the wider debate on examining – that is to say the certification of students by public examination - arguing, I think, for a very considerable reduction of the examined curriculum as a whole, and, by the same token, an expansion of the teaching and learning that, though accountable, neverthe-less would remain unexamined.

For whatever the difficulties and dangers inherent in any form of aesthetic assessment, by far the greatest damage to the central concerns of the aesthetic curriculum is wrought by the examination system. If children were simply examined or certified in a narrow range of basic skills at 16+ (for example in language and computing skills) the rest of the curriculum could be freely realigned to take full account both of the child's cultural and practical needs, and new, more appropriate and more flexible procedures for assessing and reporting progress could be devised. There is a wealth of recent experimenta-tion in these fields to draw upon once the domination of education-by-examination has been broken. As things stand however, how many arts teachers dare risk the consequence of denying the realities of the situation? If your subject is unexamined you are relegated to the ranks of the academic "left-overs" – you become educational swill that gets no recognition and no reward. Parents withdraw their children, the children withdraw their commitment and colleagues regard your work as so much garbage. But with the examination system largely dismantled (i.e. two or three subjects at 16+ and *nothing else*) the pressure would be off and educational principle might once again be re-asserted as the basis of curriculum development. What chance there is of such a thing must remain an open question. Certainly the prognostications are not good at the present time – but "policy" may eventually have to be refashioned as the inadequacy of present provision is brought home in mounting personal and public disaffection. Meanwhile one suspects that the profit-making enterprise that is our gargantuan examination system will continue to roll on as the obliging servant of vested interest, like Goya's giant eating up our children.

One of the upshots of what I have called the "tyranny" of the examination system is that in the aesthetic area we have very few really appropriate and acceptable devices for assessing children's progress. A survey of existing tests in this field carried out by Karen Moloney for the APU revealed that there was little material currently available which the Aesthetic Group might find useful, and that although many tests dealt more or less adequately with the areas of, for example, sensory discrimination and knowledge about works of art and the lives of artists, there was nothing extant of any value in the assessment of what I have called in this essay, sensibility. Moloney recommended as a general principle that "assessment in aesthetic education in the future would be best served by methods which combine the strength of an informed subjective judgement and objective description". (This is contained in the appendix of the newly published APU report on Aesthetic Development.) Tests and examinations abound: but what we lack are appropriate tests. This is at least in part a consequence of the undisputed rule of a system that is in no way geared to an evaluation of the aesthetic outcomes of education. A quick glance at a typical "O" level examination in for instance drama, with its heavy emphasis upon written work and the examination of set texts makes this clear enough. Of course the objective assessment of the skills of dramatic composition and performance is not easy – what is astonishing is that so little work has been done in this area, and my own view is that the existence of an examination system geared to non-aesthetic objectives has materially inhibited initiative in this respect. One of the benefits which might have ensued from the APU study could be the mounting of an action research programme in this area.

Although my work with adults ranges across the whole field of the arts my recent work has been largely confined to the teaching of drama and it is from this field that I will choose to exemplify my own assessment practice. In experimenting with various assessment procedures I have been concerned to try and pinpoint the factors I am really interested in and to avoid giving undue weight to the less important but perhaps more readily assessable ones. My procedure is based upon the matrix offered in Chapter 12. I have chosen lately to dispense with the sub-aesthetic category and to begin my assessment by making a general judgement of ability or competence: here I try to abstract from the particular work the student might have been doing to appraise talents and weaknesses in respect of the mode being assessed (i.e. forming, performing, etc). I then look at each element separately, give a descriptive comment in respect of a set of criteria developed to flesh out each category, and add a grade (A–E) or a mark (10–0). By averaging the marks awarded in respect of a particular batch or a period of work and placing that mark over the mark awarded for competence I get an indication of how well the students are doing in terms of their judged potential. They provide in a sense their own criteria. I have not yet involved the students in this experiment in the sense of asking them to contribute to the assessment but can see no reason why this form of appraisal should not be a joint one or why for that matter my procedure might not be adapted to form a basis of a self-evaluation inventory.

Here are the categories together with the criteria I have been using to guide my appraisals.

Category	Factors
Competence	Level of ability relative to "context". Feeling for medium. Expressiveness. Responsiveness. An over-all impression of talent as effective artistic behaviour.
Attitude	(1) Assuming the aesthetic stance – disinterested interest. (2) Sense of commitment, effort, enthusiasm – becoming absorbed. Concentration, tenacity, daring, cheerfulness, cordiality.
Discrimination	Feeling for form: timing, touch, taste, a good ear, a good eye, a sense of pace, rhythm, presence; feeling for formal qualities, for the right word, for the élan vital; perception of sign; feeling in form.
Knowledge and Technique	Mastery, range, depth, skill, finish, awareness of tradition and convention, craftsmanship, connoisseurship.
Expression	Inventiveness, flexibility, insight, impulsiveness, originality, creative process.
Imagination	Positing "fictions", alternative realities; production of images, icons.

The category "competence" gives a *holistic* impression. The following categories (including the ancillary categories related to social and language skills) are all *particular* in the sense that they are based upon a specific programme of work and assess the pupil in terms of that work. My assessment concludes with an attempt to characterize the student's work in aesthetic terms, non-judgementally. It is a purely "illuminative" device. Here are three actual examples taken from an adult class, though the names are fictitious.

Student's Name Mode:	Jenny Cantor (Age 46) Performance: R&J (Nurse)	
Competence	Little "natural" talent but works hard to achieve acceptable performances.	5 C
Attitude	Excellent; total dedication and application to the work	10 A
Skills – Expression	Intensely inhibited. Little personal inventiveness. Has to be instructed.	2 E
Discrimination	Shows only moderate sensitivity. Timing, pace, touch, all clumsy.	4 D
Imagination	Poor command of image-making – seems wary, forgetful, inconsistent.	5 C
Technique	Has few technical skills to fall back on: rather cumbersome and awkward.	4 E
Contextual Knowledge	—	—
Social Skills	Entirely adequate – serves as a good example to others. Personally rather shy and retiring.	7 B
V-C – Written	—	—
Spoken	Diffident in participating – articulate when pressed.	6 C
Characterization	Her work at its best has an integrity and natural charm that carries conviction and invites "belief". Her build makes for a rather bulky presence and cumbersome movements. Intense feeling sometimes wells up and tends to overset the performance by getting out of control. She has however a sense for the presentation of outrage, of tragedy, of injustice, idealism and suffering, combined with a curious propensity for childlike laughter.	

Student's Name Mode:	Stuart Copplestone (Age 26) Performance: R&J (Benvolio)	
Competence	A natural gift for acting – skilful and stylish, confident and able.	8 B
Attitude	Interested enough but undisciplined – expects too much help and to be indulged.	6 C
Skills – Expression	Marked lack of inventiveness – requires close directing.	6 C
Discrimination	On stage he is deft, graceful, has presence and good timing.	8 B
Imagination	Does not easily generate dramatic images though convincing within a rather narrow range when he does.	7 B
Technique	Considerable "on stage" ability – may be watched with pleasure and confidence.	9 A
Contextual Knowledge	—	—
Social Skills	Very affable and generally considerate and co-operative. Perhaps takes himself rather too seriously on occasions.	8 B
V-C Writing	—	—
Speech	A good communicator.	9 A
Characterization	Short in stature, delicate boned and featured with a trim figure: a tendency to adopt fine, gentle roles – good at expressing tender and precise feeling. Can be cool, even cold. Less convincing in more raw, more intense situations or when required to caricature. Looks very becoming – though can appear rakish, even haggard. Strong voice of considerable expressive range.	

Student's Name Mode:	Sharon Bowles (Age 36) Performance: R&J (Lady Capulet)	
Competence	Good stage presence; weakness in voice and gestural invention.	7 B
Attitude	Curiously unmotivated and unaccepting of criticism. Perhaps plagued by other problems.	5 C

Skills: Expression	Intensely diffident – rather closed, uninventive and inflexible. Inhibited.	2 E
Discrimination	Elegant and subtle playing once in possession of a text. Good stage instincts.	8 B
Imagination	Adds little beyond basic material. Needs a lot of pushing.	5 C
Technique	Whether natural or acquired most of her skills are more than competent.	9 A
Contextual Knowledge	—	—
Social Skills	Adequate, gets on well with people by and large – a strong personality responds to strong handling.	8 B
V-C Writing	—	—
Speech	A happy and effective conversationalist.	8 B
Characterization	She has good build, fine features, is poised, agile and feline. Voice best in lower register, some weakness there that rather inhibits her physical performance. Generates little presence. Feeling for cruelty, irony, and wit, but no emotional fire. Not particularly sensual.	

As I say, this is, at present, something of a personal experiment and I doubt whether all the comments entered into my inventory could be passed on directly to the student, certainly not without some sort of explanation or rider attached. However I can see that it would not be difficult to develop a "convivial" procedure based upon it, one that would allow for and include the judgments of a range of implicated individuals. Furthermore, although I have drawn my illustration from only one art form (drama) and confined my assessment to only one mode (performing) I don't think colleagues in other related fields will have too much difficulty in evaluating the scheme in their own terms or in judging its application across a wider range of operations. For all that assessment in the arts remains a fraught and contentious area I feel that we must be seen to be taking the accountability issue seriously. If we don't, we cannot expect to be taken very seriously ourselves.

CHAPTER 14

Sensual Knowledge

In aesthetic education we seek to develop sensible being – perhaps what D.H. Lawrence called "sensual knowledge". All experiences involving sensibility are life-enhancing in that they stimulate what the biologist J.Z. Young calls "the life programmes of the brain". There can be no art committed to the values of evil and death – making art is placing good things in the world. Aesthetic education is education of the poetic spirit – dedicated to the creative principle in human life. An aesthetic education educates the whole person, the reasoning heart.

★   ★   ★   ★   ★

I have in the course of writing this essay been in the habit of beginning a new section with a quotation. It has been quite an accidental procedure but has proved a most helpful aid in the process of composition. I have not exactly had to search about for the pieces I have used: they have rather "come to hand". Of course I have for some time been familiar with each of them but I never thought to use them in quite this way or to make a pattern of them. But I think that is what I have done. As I have said, each has been in its own way a touchstone for me, providing an image that at one and the same time focused thought and confirmed feeling. I have rather hesitated over using my last piece, not least because, though it seems to have lain in wait for me, I was at first unsure quite how it might signify. And then it is also rather long. But it is very beautiful and as it begins to offer so much I think I may trust it and safely go ahead. This poem more than any other of the icons I have used (Spencer's river, Berger's field, the bodger) *presented* itself to me. In as much as despite knowing the collection of poems quite well and loving many of them very much, this particular one was still something of a stranger. But I think it may well prove to be the "perfect" stranger, offering itself, disclosing itself at the very moment of my own readiness to receive it. I say the collection is by now well known to me. I had found it remaindered in a second-hand bookshop and bought it because the poet, Thomas Blackburn, had once, many years ago, visited my house and I had listened to him reading. The occasion made a deep and lasting impression upon me. This particular poem strikes me as quintessentially his and it confirms now my

141

sense then of close affinity. What is more to the point it will serve to give heart, to give a true cordiality, to these concluding paragraphs. The title of the poem is *Hallowed* – and to hallow of course means to make holy, to sanctify, to bless. A network of entomological connections links the word holy with the words hail, healthy and whole in our language – all of them concepts of central concern to any discussion of the aesthetic. Here is the poem then in full.

Hallowed

I could look from that window dawn and noon
And watch the scree shoots of the mountainside,
Whether in brightness or in massive rain,
With joy for the most part but in part afraid
Of the intensity of my looking as if
To stand against such seeing we are not made;
Since I become what I have scope and sight of,
Like being one yet also everything,
Myself in a chair and a particular stone,
Or sheen of grasses over-casting shale,
So there's no meaning in my being alone
Or any truth but what I see to tell.

I don't mind though living in Putney here,
Not seeing the mountain clarity of stars
And a certain over-used quality of the air,
Since I follow, as well as I can, that which occurs
And find a curious loving in what's near
Like letters in the morning and the smell
Of Watney's brewery sluiced in with the Thames,
And each first morning wanton with bird-call:
All occult underneath their temporal signs.

Early I am, and watch the dark thin out
In skeins of light generated from the East,
Three hundred miles from that mountain called the Knight:
But I'm here you know and still in that north west
Of feeding air. One is imagination,
Not as a gloss on facts or wished for haven,
But what all facts and livings rest upon,
The veritable metaphors of heaven.

(from *Post Mortem*, by Thomas Blackburn, Rondo Publications 1977)

The poem has such calm and such assurance. The thought moves gently yet irresistibly, gathering strength as it goes, eventually to issue in a revelatory line that transcends and yet consummates all that has gone before. Like

Berger, Blackburn is talking about "seeing" and about the mystery at the heart of perception which not only links us with all around us so we see "the proportions of our own life" there but actually identifies us with the objective world

"Like being one yet also everything."

So much of what I have been trying to write about Blackburn has caught up into this poem. He confesses to feeling

"... in part afraid
Of the intensity of my looking as if
To stand against such seeing we are not made."

Here we have again that sense of being overwhelmed by one's own experience which is part, I am sure, of the impulse to share. We feel about to burst and look about almost desperately for someone to help us earth our excitement, our agitation. For someone to give it to, someone to reflect it back to us, to bear witness to our transfiguration. Blackburn reminds us that this is the power that lives in the "poetic" perception of all things – even homely things like the smell of a brewery, like letters arriving in the morning – if you follow, as well as you can, that which occurs, you will find "a curious loving in what's near". All things then, as another poet, Gerard Manley Hopkins, was continually saying, the awesome and the trifling, the sublime and the mundane. Provided always that you attend to them, follow them as well as you can. The echo of Spencer too is surely very strong here.

And as I said it is not just that these things are in themselves interesting, wonderful and delightful though of course that is how it all starts. They become in a very real sense a part of the perceiver. For as Blackburn says, we are what we see: the subjective world is made up of all we see and do and towards which we feel and respond.

"So there's no meaning in my being alone
Or any truth but what I see to tell"

I am my sons, my daughter, my father, my wife. I am my friends, my home, the hills and fields through the window. I am that latch upon the five-barred gate, the hawk hovering over the moor, the remnants of a blackbird scattered upon the lawn, John Donne's poems, Turner's misty train. How can I be other – what else is there to be but the one whom these encounters and these feelings constitute? When Donne wrote "Every man's death diminishes me" he didn't simply mean that in causing us grief and pain the death of another cuts us down a little, reminds us of our own mortal destiny. I believe he meant quite literally that we are made less by the deaths of those who were once there for us, for whom we were and can now no longer be. Likewise every new birth, every regeneration, recovery, revelation, enlarges us, reintegrates and enriches us by making us that much more the man we might possibly become: a uniquely sensible being.

Blackburn gathers up Putney and the Welsh mountains into a single experience through the imaginative activity of his own mind, in the sensibility which houses them. Imagination he says is one (the phrase like others in the poem has a subtle ambiguity) – imagination is whole, makes one, makes holy. And one is constituted in one's imagination. Like Spencer, Blackburn would claim that heaven is now, is here, is the visible material world, and that imagination is the transfiguring faculty of the mind that gives us full access to it. In claiming that aesthetic perception is a hallowing, a sanctifying act, Blackburn is confirming much of what I have been after in writing this essay and his use of the word "veritable" with its colloquial surface and covert literal meaning, brings us full-circle. We began by looking at the otherness of art – we maintained that the arts were concerned with the truth but that their approach, in Meeson's (1981) words, was "not of the kind which aims to create conceptual structures of the world and then to harden such structures into fixed measuring points". No discussion of the function of the aesthetic in education can afford to avoid the complex question of values – and it *is* a very complex one. One would suppose that in advocating a place for the arts in education we would want to make some such claim as I have made earlier: that, like Guinness or some other cordial, the arts are good for you. Are we saying that all art is necessarily good? Are we saying that art in practice is on the side of the angels? Do we seriously want to make the claim that the experience of art is infallibly benevolent? There is a clear sense in which the Blackburn poem, equating as it does the imaginative perception of the material world with the experience of spiritual benediction, does indeed make such a claim. If we are to be able to accept this view ourselves then we must spend a moment or two trying to iron out some of the awkwardnesses that tend to confound the issue.

In maintaining that the aesthetic impulse is intrinsically good I have leant heavily upon its role as life-enhancing. I have contrasted the idea of the aesthetic with the well-known effect of an anaesthetic – something that dulls sense to the point of insensibility, obliterates consciousness, denies us both "scope and sight". Life itself, survival, depends upon the vigour of our sensible responses, the strength of our heart, and I have proposed an invigorating and cordial function for the aesthetic inasmuch as I would expect as definitive of any and every aesthetic encounter, such qualities as the arousal of sensibility and, consequent upon that arousal, the enlarging and reintegrating of consciousness itself. This is, I am aware, close to saying that aesthetic experience is basically sensuous pleasure, but I don't want to adopt that line since I am proposing, not simply pleasure, but purposeful engagement in the interests of self-knowledge and self-development. All experiences involving the engagement of sensibility are life-enhancing in that they stimulate what J.Z. Young (1980) has called the "life programmes of the brain". More than that of course – as Young has said – they feed directly into our value and belief systems without which we would be quite unable to function effectively. Here we are close to Maslow's notion of the self-actualizing person and Winnicott's claim that we are all of us creative personalities, designed to go on advancing our level of personal integration.

At the heart of aesthetic perception, as we have seen, is the capacity to discern structure, order, coherence – and this restless seeking after meaning is of itself reason enough for endorsing the aesthetic encounter. Aesthetic experience is then in the first place the experience of organization and of order – in other words, of structure. So the study of structuring becomes of central importance to us (and incidentally, though beyond the scope of this present essay, the work of the structuralist school, of very considerable relevance.) Aesthetic judgements are about the quality of structures: whether they are weak or strong, clumsy or graceful, well-adapted or makeshift and so forth. The aesthetic is the basis of all our perceptions of coherence. The enemy of the aesthetic is not, as is commonly thought, the ugly, but rather the habitual, the repetitious, the imposing; all that dulls, enervates, puts us back to sleep, drains off or curbs the vital spirit. The principle of aesthetic education is vitality, and the characteristic qualities of our work will be freedom, courage, curiosity, mischievousness, exuberance, passion, cordiality, conviviality, love, ecstasy. In this spirit we encounter the charming and the repulsive, the thrilling and the horrifying, the best and the worst. But always to make sense of them and so assimilate them into our own sensible being. So we can both own the world, in the sense of not having to reject or disown it, and in the process gain in soulfulness. Art goes beyond the merely integrative operations of sensibility to exploit the symbolic, the imaginative aspect of passionate perception. Passion (in the fashioning of materials and in the contemplating of the material world) becomes a dimension of intelligence itself, with its own way of signing the truth, and imagination renders all facts and livings "the veritable metaphors of heaven".

So we will confront the bogy, the slime, the grime, the sinister, but neither to endorse it nor to distort it – rather to assimilate it. If I do indeed become "what I have scope and sight of " there is a clear sense in which I have to become the shadow as well as the figure, the darkness as well as the light. And we are saying that such an assimilation is good. Not in the sense that by assimilating the world unto ourselves and constantly reintegrating our inner being, we are thereby bound to *act* morally or productively or wisely in the world. That is to make an overweening claim, quite beyond our scope. Rather we will have empowered sensibility. We will, if you like, have tuned

and fuelled the engine, without which, of course, there can be no action of
any kind. We will have tuned up the desire and the drive to live well. Our
actions will be good as they will be quick: life-biased. There will be life worth
the living. But there will be other filters and systems that must help give form
to that vital feeling. Arts teachers may well want to take their responsibilities
further and as educators, say to their children, "Here is the staff of life and
this is what you must do with it". But we need first of all to recognize that
there are two different occasions here. Art is neutral in the sense that it is a
symbol system available for all kinds of good purposes: as individuals and as
members of a community, living at a particular time, facing specific problems
and opportunities, we will decide how to act in art and there will be a range of
views taken about what constitutes right action or good works at any given
time. On the other hand art is committed, in as much as the deployment of
sensibility is unavoidably positive, cohering and enlivening.

There is no such thing as an art committed to the values of death or of evil.
Art will engage with both but can do no other than endorse life and
blessedness unless it is to lose the very name of art. Not the name of good art
or of great art but the name of art itself. What might be reasonably held to
constitute the good life, or good art for that matter, will perhaps always be an
open question. But the positive endorsement of life itself as ultimate good is
beyond question, is never the issue. When it is, or should it ever be so, then
the aesthetic and art as well will cease to have any meaning or any value for
man. Until such time the acid test for any work of art and for all aesthetic
experiences will simply be "Does it make life more worth the living?" At
times it might be a bit difficult to answer with a ready and enthusiastic
affirmative, but we are not asking whether we are not sometimes saddened or
dismayed or appalled by art. We can be all these things as we can be stricken
with grief and yet feel in no doubt about life itself. For the only unforgiveable
sin, we are told, is despair, is hopelessness, the loss of faith in the ultimate
goodness of life, and there isn't a work of art no matter how apparently
dreadful its impact that doesn't in some sense serve the cause of life. It is the
purpose and nature of art to engage us passionately and intimately. And here
of course I readily include art of every kind, both popular and high. The
serious practitioner of the high tradition in the arts is the aesthetic counter-
part of the research scientist, the explorer, the academic scholar, committed
to the pursuit of understanding by the conventions of their calling. For all my
endorsement of the values of the popular arts as informing the spirit and
practice of a truly comprehensive arts education I would nevertheless
strenuously wish to promote encounters with all the arts and all artists as part
of my work in the arts with children. Art is always a close encounter and its
tendency is upward, is spiritual as Kandinsky said, towards life values, love,
liberation, freedom.

The aesthetic is then on the side of life. The use we make of our aesthetic faculties will be determined by many factors: by our intelligence, our personality, our values, our attitudes, our ambitions, the constraints imposed upon us by our material and social environments. It seems reasonable to say however that despite the degree of moral neutrality that I have allowed the arts, the educational value of art would seem to lie absolutely in the area of life-enhancement and of what I have called cordiality. We are not in the business of simply informing our students about the nature of art as an activity and of its psychological and social functions. I am saying that there is nothing neutral about the arts in education which is why our criteria must be overt and open to the appraisal of others. And that means that if we choose life-enhancement and cordiality we will need to examine practice upon this basis and the development of our students in terms of their maturing sensibilities. Not forgetting that it is one of the functions of sensibility to posit a system of symbolic representation rooted in what Bernard Kaplan (in Smith & Franklyn, 1979) has called "body movement or mobilisation of the body".

This is perhaps the single, most important consequence of returning the body in education. The evoking of expressive significance, of what we have called the poetic sign, is the immediate upshot of a passionate perception. It is the representational function of feeling. In such spontaneous transformations we uncover the roots of art. It is our capacity to feel deeply and intelligently that art nourishes. The arts belong within an aesthetic education devoted to the enhancement of life through the qualification of sensibility. Body and Soul. A truly aboriginal education.

> "It was by seeing all things alert in the throb of interrelated passional significance that the ancients kept the wonder and the delight in life, as well as the dread and the repugnance. They were like children: but they had the force, the power and the *sensual knowledge* of true adults. They had a world of valuable knowledge, which is utterly lost to us." (D.H. Lawrence, *Etruscan Places*)

Endangered yes: but not yet quite lost.

Bibliography

Armstrong, Robert Plant (1975) *Wellspring*, California University Press.
Bachelard, Gaston (1958) *The Poetics of Space*, Beacon Press.
Berger, John (1980) *About Seeing*, Writers and Readers.
Blackburn, Thomas (1977) *Post Mortem*, Rondo Publications.
Coult, Tony and Kershaw, Baz (1983) *Engineers of the Imagination*, Methuen.
Denton, David (1974) *Existentialism and Phenomenology in Education*, Teachers College Press.
D.E.S. (1981) *The School Curriculum*, HMSO.
D.E.S. (1983) *Aesthetic Development*, A.P.U.
Ehrenzweig, Anton (1967) *The Hidden Order of Art*, Weidenfeld and Nicolson.
Gardner, Howard (1973) *The Arts and Human Development*, Wiley.
Gombrich, Ernst (1980) *The Sense of Order*, Phaidon.
Gulbenkian Foundation (1982) *The Arts in Schools*.
Hebdige, Dick (1979) *Subculture*, Methuen.
Johnstone, Keith (1981) *IMPRO*, Eyre Methuen.
Jones, David (1959) *Epoch and Artist*, Faber.
Kandinsky, Wassily (1977) *Concerning the Spiritual in Art*, Dover Publications.
Kivy, Peter (1980) *The Corded Shell*, Princeton University Press.
Lawrence, D.H. (1952) *Etruscan Places*, Penguin Books.
Leach, Edmund (1976) *Culture and Communication*, Cambridge University Press.
Marcuse, Herbert (1979) *The Aesthetic Dimension*, Papermac.
Margolis, Joseph (1980) *Art and Philosophy*, Humanities Press.
Massingham, H.J. (1939) *The English Countryside*, Batsford.
Meeson, Philip (1981) *Arts as Symbol or Thing*, British Journal of Aesthetics, Vol. 21, No. 1.
Persig, Robert (1976) *Zen and the Art of Motorcycle Maintenance*, Corgi.
Polanyi, M. and Prosch, H.P. (1976) *Meaning*, Routledge and Kegan Paul.
Reid, Louis Arnaud (1969) *Meaning in the Arts*, Allen and Unwin.
Ross, Malcolm (1975) *The Arts and the Adolescent*, Evans Methuen.
Ross, Malcolm (1978) *The Creative Arts*, Heinemann Educational Books.
Ross, Malcolm (1980) *The Arts and Personal Growth*, Pergamon Press.
Ross, Malcolm (1981) *The Aesthetic Imperative*, Pergamon Press.
Ross, Malcolm (1982) *The Development of Aesthetic Experience*, Pergamon Press.
Ross, Malcolm (1983) *The Arts: A Way of Knowing*, Pergamon Press.
Smith, Nancy R. and Franklyn, Margery B. (1979) *Symbolic Functioning in Childhood*, Lawrence Erlbaum Associates.
Steiner, George (1969) *Language and Silence*, Penguin Books.
Turner, V.W. (1974) *The Ritual Process*, Penguin Books.
Vernon, P. (1970) *Creativity*, Penguin Books.
Williams, R. (1976) *Key Words*, Fontana.
Willis, P. (1978) *Profane Culture*, Calder.
Winnicott, D.W. (1971) *Playing and Reality*, Tavistock.
Witkin, R.W. (1974) *The Intelligence of Feeling*, Heinemann Educational Books.
Wollheim, Richard (1979) *The Sheep and the Ceremony*, Cambridge University Press.
Young, J.Z. (1980) *Programs of the Brain*, Cambridge University Press.

Author Index